DONATION

2390379

The V&A Book of

Western Ornament

J. Berain Inuenit et delineauit   D   Doliuar Sculpsit

The V&A Book of

Western Ornament

Michael Snodin

V&A Publications

First published by V&A Publications, 2006
V&A Publications
Victoria and Albert Museum
South Kensington
London SW7 2RL

Distributed in North America by Harry N. Abrams, Inc., New York

ISBN 10 1 85177 472 6
ISBN 13 978185177 472 2

Library of Congress Control Number 2005935063

10 9 8 7 6 5 4 3 2 1
2009 2008 2007 2006 2005

A catalogue record for this book is available from the British Library.

Designed by Caroline and Roger Hillier, The Old Chapel Graphic Design
New V&A Photography by Richard Davis and Paul Robins, V&A Photographic Studio

Front jacket illustrations: roundel, Italian, *c.*1510 (p.69); detail of border from *The Grammar of Ornament* (p.15); model of a tomb at Palmyra (p.39)
Back jacket illustration: detail of lace border, Italian, *c.*1600–25 (p.21)
Half-title page: gold-tooled calf binding, 1643 (p.61)
Frontispiece: a grotesque, French, *c.*1685–93 (p.75)
Title page: model, based on Bramante's Tempietto (p.41)

Printed in Hong Kong

V&A Publications
Victoria and Albert Museum
South Kensington
London SW7 2RL
www.vam.ac.uk

FOREWORD

This book springs from the V&A's Gallery of European Ornament, which opened in the Henry Cole Wing in 1992 and closed in 2004. The gallery was curated by myself, Hilary Young, Clare Graham and Maurice Howard, who worked under the staff exchange scheme between the V&A and the University of Sussex. The whole team contributed to the gallery narrative on which the book is based and to the selection of objects, about one third of which are used to tell the story here. Maurice Howard and Clare Graham also contributed to the gallery texts. To all of them I am profoundly grateful.

Michael Snodin
July 2005

INTRODUCTION

For thousands of years people have decorated or ornamented themselves and the things around them. This book looks at the ornament used in Europe and North America over the past 500 years. Up to about 100 years ago ornament played a leading role in the design of many things, from cathedrals to coffee pots. Today, although less prominent than it was, ornament surrounds us still: inside and outside our homes, on clothes and household objects, even on cars and aeroplanes. Many ornamental motifs are very ancient and others more modern, but most have been used for more than their design appeal. For behind the human desire to decorate lies the need to give some special meaning to the things we make.

This book begins by looking at how and why we use ornament, and at the way in which ornamental ideas have travelled from place to place and across the centuries. It then examines ornament that originates in simple geometrical lines and circles or borrows ideas from the human form and the natural world. It goes on to describe the ornament based on the architecture of ancient Greece and Rome, which dominated European design from about 1450 to the mid-twentieth century. Finally, the book examines ornament that looks back to the European Middle Ages or out beyond the Western world. Most of the illustrations are taken from the collections of the Victoria and Albert Museum, the world's largest museum of decorative art, a vast treasure-house of ornament waiting to be explored.

MOUNTAIN BLUE BIRD
British, 1959
Designed and modelled by
Dorothy Doughty
Made by the Royal Worcester
Porcelain Company
Bone china painted in enamel
colours
C.142–1963 (Bequeathed by the
artist through Miss F.G. Doughty)
This object has immediate appeal as 'an ornament' for the home, both in its realism and in the way it captures a rare and beautiful piece of the natural world.

What is ornament?

The word 'ornament' is often used to describe a small decorative object. 'An ornament' for the mantelshelf may make us wonder at its realism or the skill with which it was made, but it is not at all functional. But 'ornament' can also mean decoration and decorative motifs in the widest sense; this kind of ornament is the subject of this book. Some things that look like household items may be decorated in such a way that they become impractical and so are classed as 'ornaments'. A nineteenth-century commemorative plate, for example, may be so crowded with decoration as to be essentially a display or 'sideboard' piece and not for everyday use. Many of the decorative ideas or motifs found on objects such as this have been copied so often and so widely that we take them for granted. Yet many of them originated thousands of years ago, when they had special meanings and were used only in certain places.

DISH

British, about 1855
Painted by Thomas Kirkby
Made by Minton & Co.
Earthenware, painted in enamel colours
3340–1856

The South Kensington Museum (the future Victoria and Albert Museum) purchased this dish from the International Exhibition in Paris in 1855,when it was also collecting Italian Renaissance maiolica. With its grotesque ornament and a bust of Queen Victoria in profile, the dish consciously imitates sixteenth-century maiolica examples.

BARREL-JUG

Cypriot, 7th century BC
Found in a tomb at Gastria
Painted earthenware
222–1883

Pottery has been decorated almost from the moment of its invention. This pot, which was made about 2,700 years ago, uses patterns taken from Greek pottery in the 'geometric' style.

CANDELABRUM
British, London hallmarks for 1810–11
Mark of Paul Storr; engraved with the Ormonde crest
Silver
M.52–1982
Motifs from ancient Greek and Roman architecture are here adapted to a quite different object, but they retain their original decorative meaning.

LOTUS-PATTERN WALLPAPER
British, the design registered
23 June 1858
Designed by Owen Jones
Colour print from wood blocks
8342.41
Wallpapers, with their flat, repeated patterns, are the ornament of wall surfaces. The basic motif of the repeat is taken from one of the most common forms in ancient Egyptian design.

Ornament and function

Ornament is often more than just decorative. It can, for instance, turn an object into a symbol or sign. The Lalique mascot, for example, symbolizes speed, even when removed from its place on a car bonnet. Sometimes the method of manufacture and the needs of design come together to provide appropriate ornament. The very process of making can also create ornament: the ridges on a helmet both strengthen the metal and decorate the plain steel, while the potter may leave evidence of finger trails in the wet clay of a vase. Equally, ornament can be used to trick the eye by covering up the function, as on the sewing machine. Surprisingly, some seemingly functional designs can have more to do with ornament than you might at first think, as the shoes and car wheel trim show.

SEWING MACHINE
British, about 1875–92
Designed and made in London by
Edward Ward
Cast iron with enamelled
decoration
M.44–1991 (Maja Schalburg
Bequest)
The functional demands of a sewing machine do not result in an easy or regular shape for decoration, yet the side facing the operator is covered with ornament, unlike the back, which is plain. Such decoration was essential if the machine was to be part of a Victorian domestic interior.

BREAD OR CAKE BASKET
British, London hallmark for 1771–2
Mark of Richard Mills
Silver
M.1696–1944
The basket echoes an ancient Greek shape, and the wheat motif symbolizes the nature of the contents for which it was designed.

VASE
British, about 1924
Designed and made by Reginald Wells at the Soon Pottery, Storrington, West Sussex
Stoneware with opaque, crackled white glaze
C.60–1925 (Given by Sir Amhurst Selby-Bigge, Ernest Marsh and Bernard Rackham)
The rings produced by the potter's fingers as he threw the pot on the wheel have been made into a decorative feature, as has the cracking of the glaze in the kiln.

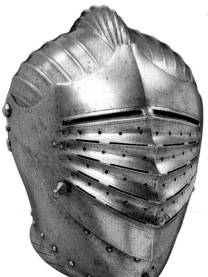

CLOSE HELMET WITH FLUTED SKULL
Probably Austrian, about 1510–20
Possibly by Konrad Seusenhofer, who worked at Innsbruck
Steel
M.195–1921
The strengthening ridges along the top of the helmet, the holes across the face and the rivets at the bottom all serve a practical purpose, but their arrangement makes patterns and thus also ornaments the piece.

'SPIRIT OF THE WIND' CAR MASCOT

French, about 1930
Made by Lalique
Cast glass
Circ.199–1972

A symbol of speed whether on or off the car, this mascot extends the technique of glass-making to give the effect of wind-blown hair. This type of mascot was designed to be illuminated. In France this mascot was also called 'Victoire'.

CAR WHEEL TRIM

British, 1991
Designed for the Vauxhall Astra MK 2 made from 1984
Plastic and steel
M.9–2005 (Given by Vauxhall Motors Ltd)

Fuel-saving aerodynamic design means that there are very few ways to add ornament to the modern car. Wheel trims reduce drag, dirt and road noise, but their chief purpose is to add a distinctive decorative touch to a plain body, at the same time as showing off the manufacturer's name. In this trim the badge in the centre shows a griffin, taken from the coat of arms of the company, which was originally that of its parent, the Vauxhall Iron Works.

PAIR OF 'INSTRUCTOR MID ERS' AEROBIC SHOES

British, 1991
Made in East Asia for Reebok UK
Leather upper and synthetic materials
T.140:1+2-1991 (Given by Reebok UK)

Ornament and function often overlap in the design of sports footwear. In these shoes the wavy line defines the place of the ankle, but continues as ornament. As a high-status object intended for aerobics instructors, the shoes have soles designed to be seen during the activity: they show the decorative pattern of the treads, air tubes of the 'Energy Return System' and the trademark. The ventilation holes are concealed by an almost architectural arched motif.

Prints and ornament

From about 1500 improvements in techniques of production and cheaper paper meant that printed images became widely circulated. Prints of ornament enabled Europe to share a common range of popular designs, transmitting ideas and motifs across great distances. The long history of many designs is evident in the repetitions of the same print published in different countries at different times. Prints were sold and distributed by booksellers and often came in sets. Ornament prints were also used to teach drawing to students, first in artists' and manufacturers' workshops and later in academies and schools of art. Copying standard motifs from prints became the way by which students proved their level of competence. Prints were also used as a mechanical means of producing ornament, for instance in fabric design. In the late nineteenth century, examinations set by the Department of Science and Art, based at the Victoria and Albert Museum, demanded that candidates draw ornamental motifs from plaster casts rather than prints, placed under a direct light for strong shadows.

below
VASE
French, early 18th century
Probably made in Dieppe
Ivory with a silver finial; the two handles and base are later additions
32–1917 (Bequeathed by H.L. Florence)
Finely worked versions of the Bartoli print were made in expensive materials to please discriminating collectors.

Vaso cinerario trouato nel cauo di
un gran masso di fabrica antica
fuori la Porta Salara.

PRINT OF A VASE
Italian, 1697
By Pietro Santo Bartoli
Engraving
17239
This print records an important example of late Roman art, a marble cinerary urn found in a tomb on the Via Appia Antica in Rome, making its design available for copying in various forms and media. It was the most influential of all the vase prints in Bartoli's important record of Roman remains, *Gli antichi sepolcri, overo mausolei . . .* , which was reissued five times up to 1768.

top

TITLE-PAGE FOR A SET OF FRIEZES

Italian, 1628

By Odoardo Fialetti after Polifilio Giancarli

Engraving

17484

This set of prints, which was published in Rome, helped to spread Italian Baroque scrolling ornament to France, Britain and the Netherlands.

middle

TITLE-PAGE FOR A SET OF FRIEZES

French, 1646

After Odoardo Fialetti

Engraving

E.761–1927

Here the original Italian set or an Amsterdam version of 1636, has been copied in Paris. It is described as being suitable for painters, sculptors, cabinetmakers and others.

bottom

TITLE-PAGE FOR A SET OF FRIEZES

English, 1672

By William Vaughan after Odoardo Fialetti

Engraving

28199.1

The set originating in 1628 was copied in England nearly half a century after the original. With time and repeated copying, the design has become smaller and cruder in execution.

PRINT OF A RAFFLE LEAF

British, 1753
By Henry Copland, from the set A New Book of Ornaments *very necessary for the instruction of those unacquainted with that useful part of drawing*
Engraving
28389.10

This print was made as an example for students to copy (see below). It develops the skill of broadening and thinning the drawn line to suggest shading and turning in space. The raffle leaf, a version of the ancient Greek and Roman acanthus, was an essential part of the decorative repertoire of the eighteenth-century craftsman.

A RAFFLE LEAF

British, about 1760
After Henry Copland
Pen and ink and wash
D.839–1906

This is a typically competent student's copy, probably drawn by an apprentice craftsman. Copland's set of prints was reissued about 1768.

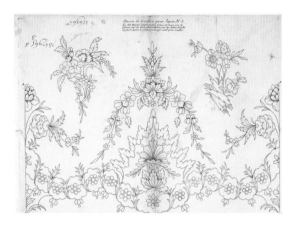

PRINTED EMBROIDERY PATTERN FOR A PETTICOAT

French, 1760s
Published by Daudet of Lyon
Etching
E.761–1912

This print would have been placed directly onto the cloth, pricked, and pounced through. The resulting line of dots on the cloth would then be connected together by drawing. A continuous frieze of pattern could be made simply by repeating the process.

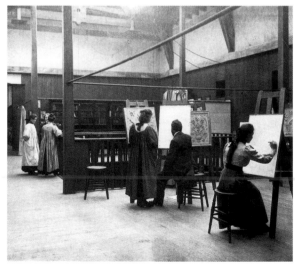

PHOTOGRAPH BY THOMAS ANNAN OF A DRAWING CLASS AT THE GLASGOW SCHOOL OF ART
About 1900
The female students at the Glasgow School of Art are shown drawing from relief casts set up on easels.
Photograph courtesy of the Glasgow School of Art Collection

Ornament becomes official

The Department of Science and Art, which ran the newly founded museums at South Kensington, London (including the future V&A), in the 1850s, was an arbiter of design and oversaw the nation's art education. It supplied art teachers via a network of training schools, lent books from the National Art Library and set the national curriculum in design training, much of which was focused on the teaching of ornament. The National Art Library contained a huge range of ornament books, while the Museum also spread the message through making and showing copies and casts of ornament in three dimensions.

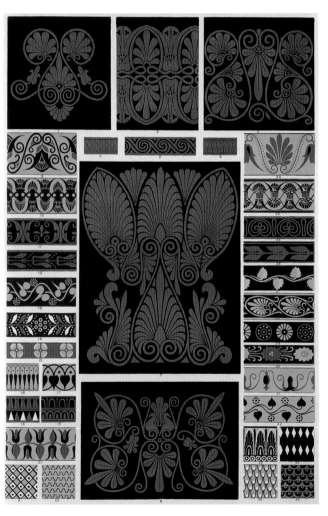

PAGE FROM *THE GRAMMAR OF ORNAMENT*
1856
Owen Jones
49 G 54
The Grammar of Ornament is the best known of the great published compendiums of ornament that played a central role in design in mid-nineteenth century. It was the first standard history of world ornament, arranged systematically according to a set of 'general principles'. Thanks to its bright lithographed plates, it was also a practical design source book. This page, 'Greek No 5', shows painted patterns on ancient Greek vases in the British Museum and the Louvre.

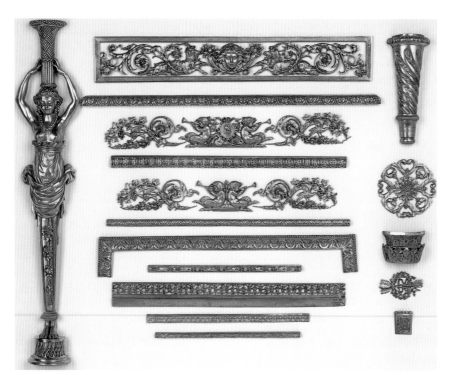

SET OF COPIES OF GILT-BRONZE FURNITURE MOUNTS

British, about 1877
Made by Elkington and Co. of Birmingham after a set of mounts probably made by François Remond of Paris
Electrotypes in gilt and silvered copper 1877–39

Electrotype copies and plaster casts of architectural details and historic objects were commissioned by the South Kensington Museum, the forerunner of the V&A. They were for sale, but were also displayed in the Museum and circulated to art schools. This set records all the ormolu ornament on a French commode of about 1785, thought in 1877 to have been made by Pierre Gouthière. It was lent to art schools between 1928 and 1955.

TWO STUDIES OF A SOW THISTLE

British, about 1850
By Richard Redgrave
Reproduced in his Manual of Design, *1876*
Pen and ink
8452.A&B (Given by A. Reid in 1879)
From about 1840 to 1900 there was great interest in deriving ornament from plants. These drawings by Redgrave, an influential teacher in the Government School of Design, show the thistle 'pictorially drawn as it grows' and 'displayed and flattened . . . the form of the buds, the open blossoms, the seed vessels and the leaves are examined as new motives for ornament'.

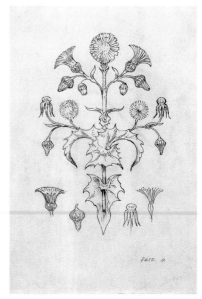

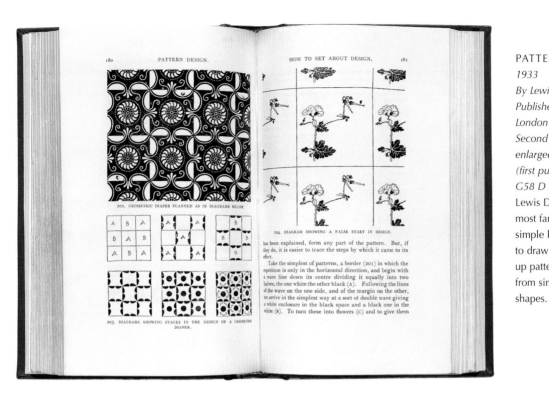

PATTERN DESIGN
1933
By Lewis F. Day
Published by B.T. Batsford,
London
Second edition, revised and
enlarged by A. Penn, 1933
(first published in 1903)
G58 D 66

Lewis Day's books were the most famous examples of simple handbooks of how to draw ornament, building up pattern as an evolution from simple to complex shapes.

CAST OF A GOTHIC CAPITAL
British, early 19th century
Plaster
A.1916–250

This cast is taken from a thirteenth-century capital in a nave window at Westminster Abbey. In the nineteenth century plaster casts of architectural ornament played an important role in the education of architects, designers and craftsmen. This capital was in the private museum of medieval art formed about 1825 by the architect and antiquary Lewis Nockalls Cottingham. In the 1850s it became the basis of the Architectural Museum housed in the complex of museums at South Kensington.

ORNAMENT AND GEOMETRY

Lines, diaper and chequer

A line is the most basic form of ornament. It is often used, either straight or formed as a band of continuously repeated motifs, to emphasize the shape of an object. This is especially true of the linear decoration cut into the surfaces of objects by machines. In clothing the human body, lines have often been used to bring out the contour and shape of the limbs beneath, as have design features such as stitching or applied ornament. Patterns of crossing lines, such as chequer or the diamonds of diaper work, can sometimes help us to see shapes, but they can also be used to break them down. The eye is invited to follow different paths across the surface, reading it as a series of squares here, a series of lozenge shapes there, giving variety, or even making us uncertain what the object is.

GOBLET
Italian, 19th century
Made in Venice
Latticino glass
Circ.434–1927
One of the chief decorative characteristics of glass is the possibility of showing ornament within the body of the material itself. Here the netlike pattern enables us to see the shape of the bowl.

DECANTER
British or Irish, about 1820
Cut glass
Circ.392–1912
The cutting and polishing of glass into a series of facets to catch the light create a complex diaper pattern across its rounded surface.

BREAD BASKET
British, London
hallmark for 1761–2
Mark E.R.
Silver
Circ.398–1925
The great variety of pierced decorative diaper work around the edge of the basket is produced by an inexpensive mechanical process that replaced skilled hand work.

TARTAN SASH
British, about 1850
Woven silk net
T.147–1971
The overlaying of lines of colour that give a rich variety to tartan patterns have been part of textile design for thousands of years and emerge from the weaving process by which fabrics are made.

LADIES' CUSTOMIZED BIKER-STYLE JACKET
British, 1990
Designed by Sally J. Widiner
Made by Leather Technics of London
Black leather with steel ornamentation, including suitcase components and bicycle chains.
T.146–1991
Certain materials come to be associated with particular fastenings, no matter what the object. The witty design of this jacket comes through its use of metal luggage trimmings as well as its reference to bikes through chains.

BEYOND THE THRESHOLD
1929
By Jean Paul Raymond
Published by the Curwen Press, Plaistow
Translated, illustrated and bound by Charles Ricketts.
L.1818–1958
The delicate net of overlapping lines recalls the light and ephemeral painted patterns of ancient Roman wall decoration.

Circles, dots, triangles and abstraction

Geometrical ornament has been popular ever since people first tried to draw the perfect circle, experimented with the interesting shapes of intersecting triangles, or made complex patterns of carefully placed dots. The addition of colour can confuse foreground and background, or pattern and the 'field' on which it is placed. It may not be possible to tell whether one shape has been laid over another, or vice versa. Such experiments, based on the way the human eye sees things, have led to the process that we call 'abstraction', where shapes appear to have no connection with natural forms at all. Abstraction produces new ideas for such things as decorative borders and framing patterns. Twentieth-century abstract patterns have been greatly inspired by the art of so-called primitive societies, as well as the work of modern painters.

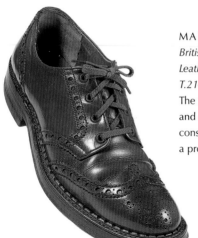

MAN'S BROGUE SHOE
British, 1940s or '50s
Leather
T.21–1983
The traditional brogue is decorated with circles and dots along the lines of the shoe's construction, emphasizing the stitching and as a prominent field pattern on the toecap.

FLOWERPOT AND STAND
British, about 1790
Made by the Wedgwood factory
Black Jasper stoneware, decorated in white
841&a–1905 (Given by J.H. Fitzhenry)
This pot was made at time when simple field patterns of dots or squares were overtaking the older figurative or floral patterns. The simple dotted pattern here is similar to that found on contemporary wallpaper and textiles, and is typical of the Neo-classical style. It still looks startlingly modern.

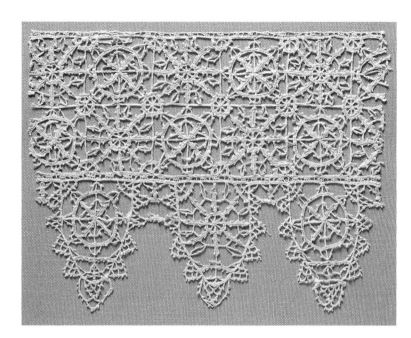

left

TIE

British, late 1960s
Made by Distinctive
Pattern Ties
Crepe, printed in
black, lined with
ivory silk, and
interlined with
wool.
T.328–1984
Circles here join up
and jostle each
other to create an
abstract design that
seems to be
random. The
restriction of such a
pattern to a small
but prominent item
of clothing makes
abstraction
acceptable to
consumers with
conservative taste.

LACE BORDER

Italian, about
1600–25
Reticella *and*
punto in aria
T.275–1912
Intricate geometric
patterns are here
created in lace:
placed against a
dark backing, the
positive/negative
effects of pattern
on ground are
brought out.

PLATE

British, about 1972
Designed by Eduardo Paolozzi
Made by Wedgwood
Bone china with printed decoration
Circ.512e–1972
One of a set of six Paolozzi plates entitled 'Variations on
a Geometric Theme'. The effect of a complex, multi-
sectioned surface of diagonal, zigzag and circular
patterns has been created with the appropriately
'mechanical' aid of screen-printing, rather than the
traditional painting on ceramics.

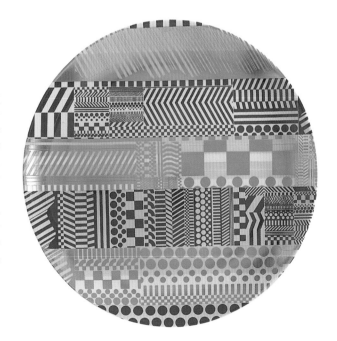

NATURAL ORNAMENT

Images and symbols

Faced with a choice of subjects, the human eye automatically picks out people and animals first. This is because primitive instincts still rule our immediate responses, telling us to watch out for possible threats and opportunities. Images of living creatures are therefore a powerful way of grabbing our attention, and have always been a popular subject for ornament. They are decorative in themselves and can also have a whole range of meanings for us. The same can be said of man-made objects. Using these meanings, we can turn creatures and objects into symbols, visible signs of abstract ideas and qualities. These can be used to build up whole languages based on pictures rather than words, as in heraldry. These languages became less important, and less familiar, as people learned to read and write. But such images remain a quick way of giving meaning and interest to our surroundings.

DOOR KNOCKER
British, about 1820
Cast iron
1007–1897 (Given by Alfred Chadwick)
The mask is that of the jovial old drunkard Silenus, nurse and attendant of the Greek wine-god Dionysus or Bacchus. It was copied from Coadestone ornaments made in the eighteenth century for decorating buildings.

People, masks and medallions

The human image is one of the oldest subjects in ornament. Its power is so great that some cultures have totally forbidden its use, seeing it as a blasphemy, an invasion of the divine power of creation. Within the Western pictorial tradition, however, classical gods and Christian saints are among the subjects most frequently used. Figures often have a symbolic purpose. This can be underlined by giving them distinctive and appropriate accessories, or attributes. Human beings instinctively focus first on the face, especially the eyes. This can make a better decorative feature than a whole figure. Detached human and animal faces or masks have been used in ornament since ancient times and derive from the masks used in ancient Greek theatre. Imitations of engraved cameos and medallions also derive from ancient Greek and Roman examples, and were especially popular with Neo-classical designers in the eighteenth century.

A CHERUB'S HEAD AND WINGS
British, early 19th century
By Jonathan Harmer
Terracotta
A.9–1919
This relief would originally have been set into a tombstone or memorial. Harmer lived in Heathfield and made many small terracotta plaques of this kind for East Sussex churches. The cherub head symbolizes Christian resurrection and salvation.

WAISTCOAT

British, 1780–1800

Striped white satin; the applied medallions are printed in black on a white satin, with embroidery in coloured silks and chenille

256–1880

All the figures in the medallions are copied from prints showing recently discovered Roman wall paintings in the famous series of books *Le antichità di Ercolano* (*Antiquities of Herculaneum*), published from 1757 to 1779. The two larger medallions below the pockets show *The Cupid Seller*, a subject much copied after its publication in 1762.

DESIGNS FOR MASKS

French, 1676

By Nicolas Robert after Georges Charmeton

Engraving

E.1173–1923

One of a series of designs for masks in the Baroque style, suitable for woodcarving, silver, ironwork and many other materials.

THE 'PROMETHEUS' VASE
British, 1867
Modelled by Victor Simyan, painted by Thomas Allen at the
Minton factory, Stoke-on-Trent
Earthenware, painted, with coloured glazes
Exhibited by Minton at the Paris Exhibition of 1867
1047–1871

This typical nineteenth-century virtuoso piece is decorated in imitation of sixteenth-century maiolica, although the base is decorated with snakes in the manner of the sixteenth-century French ceramicist Bernard Palissy. The scenes on the bowl of the vase are taken from prints after paintings by the Rubens. This vase took its name from the cover, where Prometheus is having his entrails removed by an eagle, a punishment set by Zeus for stealing fire from the gods and taking it to earth.

'SCOUT' BISCUIT TIN
British, 1911
Made by Hudson Scott & Sons for Carr & Co.
Marked: copyright 1166
Tin plate, offset litho printed
M.81–1983 (M.J. Franklin Collection)
With a portrait of Lord Baden-Powell, the founder of the Boy Scout movement, which swept the world after he published *Scouting for Boys* in 1908.

Objects and emblems

Like animals or people, man-made things are a rich source of ornament. Sometimes they are just arranged in a pattern. More often, they refer to the purpose or ownership of the object they decorate. Lettering is an obvious way to do this when people can read or write, but pictures can be a more immediate and evocative way of getting a message across. They can be used simply, or built up into complicated systems of symbolism and allegory. A good example is heraldry. Coats of arms started as simple personal badges or emblems used for identification on the battlefield. From the twelfth century onwards they were studied and regulated through much of Western Europe. Gradually they developed into an international language of symbols, flexible enough to provide a complete record of an individual's family history and achievements, and decorative enough to be used on any of his belongings.

TILE
Dutch, 17th century
Tin-glazed earthenware
C.566–1923
This tile comes from a set showing ships, used as a panel in a fireplace or on a wall. Decorative in itself, the ship also may refer to the importance of trade for the Dutch economy.

SPOON
North German, early 16th century
Silver-gilt, inset with an animal tooth and engraved
485–1865
Silver spoons were highly prized possessions in the medieval period. The decoration on this one is rich in Christian symbolism, including the instruments of Christ's Passion on the stem and the figures of the infant Christ, St Anne and the Virgin Mary on the bowl. The two female saints may have been favourite or patron saints of the owner, who was very possibly a woman. The tooth is probably intended to be a charm against disease and misfortune.

'DORSET' BISCUIT TIN
British, 1937
Made by Barringer, Wallis & Manners for Carr & Co.
Tin plate, offset litho printed
M.91–1983 (M.J. Franklin Collection)
Idyllic views of thatched country cottages have long had great sentimental appeal for the British: the view on this tin is of Thomas Hardy's birthplace at Higher Brockhampton in Dorset.

'CHAIR THING' (CHILD'S CHAIR)

British, 1968
Designed by Peter Murdoch
Made by Perspective Designs Ltd
Fibreboard printed with lettering in black on white
Circ.795–1968

This paper chair was an inexpensive but fashionable product, designed to be delivered flat for home assembly. It is decorated with lettering in a variety of typefaces, including the fancy Victorian ones that were revived in the 1950s and '60s. A spotted pattern was also available. It won a Council of Industrial Design Award in 1968.

COVER FOR THE BBC HANDBOOK

British, 1929
Designed by Edward McKnight Kauffer
Colour process engraving (proof copy)
E.1105–1965

Lightning has long been used to signify power and enlightenment. Later it became an appropriate symbol for electricity, the telegraph and other modern forms of communication.

DISH

Italian, about 1530–40
Made in Deruta
Tin-glazed and lustred earthenware
3033–1855

The dish is painted with the coat of arms of the ruling Medici family of Florence. The five golden balls or besants may refer to the origins of the family's wealth in banking, while the three fleur-de-lis (stylized lilies or irises) are on the badge of the city of Florence, forming a heraldic pun on its name. The three golden balls used as a sign by pawnbrokers are said to have been copied from the Medici arms.

Real and imaginary creatures

Our ancestors decorated their caves with paintings of the animals they hunted, and the ones who hunted them. Unconscious memories of this primitive past may account for the continuing popularity of creatures of all kinds in ornaments. They have often been used as symbols of what we think are their characteristic qualities, from the courage of the lion to the industry of the bee. Not content with the variety of nature, man has dreamt up whole worlds full of imaginary beasts in stories and legends. Some, like the dragon, seem to be based on dim recollections or rumours of real creatures. Others are strange assemblies of parts. The sphinx, for instance, joins the head of a woman to the body of a lion, sometimes adding the wings of an eagle. These unlikely creations were especially popular with designers of the grotesque in ancient Rome and the Renaissance.

SPHINX CANDLESTICK
British, about 1778–9
Derby factory
Porcelain, decorated in enamels and gilt
C.30–1975
Sphinxes were a popular subject in the eighteenth century, for both Neo-classical and Egyptian-style decoration. Both had lions' bodies. Greek and Roman sphinxes had female heads and were sometimes winged, like this example, while Egyptian sphinxes had a man's or an animal's head.

DISH
Spanish, about 1500
Valencia (possibly Manises)
Enamelled earthenware, incised and painted in copper lustre
C.2050–1910 (Salting Bequest)
As the courageous king of the beasts, the lion is probably the animal most frequently used in ornament. The formalized prancing or rampant lion on this display dish derives from Western heraldry, although the Islamic influence on Spanish ceramics at this date is also evident.

PRINT:
DESIGN FOR A SWORD HILT
French, about 1555
By Pierre Woeriot
Engraving
E.2362–1910
Imaginary creatures inspired by ancient Roman grotesques have been bent into a handle and guard for a sword.

JUG
French, 1550–1600
Made by Bernard Palissy or a follower
Lead-glazed earthenware; the gilt metal mounts are probably late 18th century
79–1865 (Pourtales Collection)

Palissy cast his ornaments from real animals and shells. This jug was originally a vase, decorated with the sort of creatures and plants that populated the artificial garden grottoes he created in French gardens.

SET OF TENNIS BALLS
USA, 1991
Made by Prince Manufacturing Inc.,
Princeton, New Jersey
Synthetic materials
T.179–1991 (Given by Michael Snodin)

Walt Disney's Mickey Mouse is the twentieth century's most famous fantasy creature. Born in 1928, he is still a potent advertising symbol.

VASE
French, about 1925
Designed by Edgar Brandt
Patinated cast bronze
M.109–1978

Edgar Brandt's metalwork was an important influence on the development of the Art Deco style in both France and the USA. It often included stylistic abstractions of natural forms: here, the central motif suggests an insect emerging from its chrysalis.

Plants and natural pattern

Plants, both real and imaginary, have always been among the most popular subjects for decoration. Nearly every major system of ornament, including classical architectural decoration, includes elements based on their forms. Their beauty and variety make them an obvious choice: as well as brightly coloured flowers, the possibilities include leaves and trees, fruit and even vegetables. They lend themselves to a wide range of decorative treatments, from careful botanical observation to almost unrecognizable abstraction, and from sprawling and luxuriant naturalism to rigidly formalized patterns. Their flexibility is equally important, since their curved stems and leaves can comfortably fill any space that needs to be decorated. This process seems so natural to our eyes that almost any curling pattern may develop into a plant, whatever its origin. Other types of natural ornament are derived from patterns that naturally occur in nature.

Plant patterns: formalization and arrangement

Stylized flowers and plants are much more common in ornament than realistic representations. Imitation is always easier than invention, and the history of traditional plant motifs like the palmette, the rosette and the acanthus in ancient Greek architectural ornament (see pp.54–9) shows flowers and leaves being copied, recopied and adapted over the centuries until they are very far removed from their originals. Technical constraints can also be decisive: weaving naturalistic flowers is not easy, although they have always been a popular subject for textiles. Deliberate simplification or abstraction can also be more decorative than realism. By concentrating on one aspect of the plant, such as the radiating pattern on a pine cone or the veins of a leaf, striking effects can be achieved. Plants arranged in vases and baskets are also popular subjects for ornament, while swags of leaves are an important element of classical decoration.

DISH
Italian, about 1520
Made in Deruta
Tin-glazed earthenware with lustre added at a final firing
1614–1856
The radiating diapered pattern suggests the base of a pine cone.

'TULIP' BISCUIT TIN
British, about 1929
Made by Hudson Scott & Sons for Peek Frean & Co
Tin plate, offset litho printed;
M.677–1983
Stylized flower arrangements were a popular motif in Art Deco ornament of the 1920s and '30s.

Plant patterns:
herbals and the sprig

The first herbals, or books of plants, were printed in the 1480s, although some had been circulating as manuscripts for many centuries before this. They were mainly intended as a guide to the medicinal and other useful properties of plants, and over the next 200 years they were produced in great numbers. The earliest illustrations were crude and sometimes inaccurate woodcuts, and although the standard improved greatly after 1530, they were always mainly intended to be schematic diagrams to help with identification rather than works of art. The usual convention was to show an uprooted plant or a broken-off shoot or sprig. Nevertheless, they became an important source of ornament, especially for embroiderers and plasterers. By placing these motifs at regular intervals against a plain background, a pretty if unassertive effect could be achieved. Sprigged patterns have remained quietly but consistently popular right up to the present day, especially for textiles and wallpapers.

TRACTATUS DE VIRTUTIBUS HERBARUM
1502
Published in Venice by
Christophorus de Pensis
87 C 100
An example of the early type of herbal with crude woodblock illustrations, open at the description of the strawberry. This book belonged to William Morris: the Arts and Crafts designers of the nineteenth century studied herbals in their search for a new style of natural ornament.

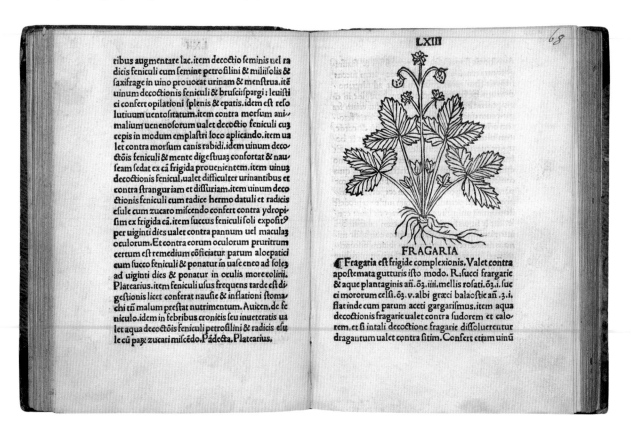

DECORATIVE PAPER
Italian, 18th century
Print from woodblocks
E.5068–1897
Here sprigs have been placed within a trellis of leaves and single flowers. This paper would have been used by a bookbinder, or as a wrapping or lining paper.

PAIR OF LADIES' EVENING SHOES
Belgian, about 1925
Labelled: 'Hand made expressly in Belgium for Lilley & Skinner Ltd., London'
Gold kid, painted and lined with grey kid
Painted with a pattern of multi-coloured sprigs
T.125&a–1962

Plant patterns: the pomegranate pattern

The pomegranate is one of the names given to the formalized plant pattern that has been popular in Europe ever since it appeared on Italian textiles in the fifteenth century. Its design principle became the basis of all drop-repeat patterns. Curving stems and leaves form regular compartments, each framing a central fruit or flower-head. This can look like a pomegranate, a pine cone, a pineapple or an artichoke. All these names have been used to describe it, but it seems to have started life as an entirely imaginary creation with no symbolic significance. The pattern probably developed from Indian Tree of Life designs, by way of imported Islamic silks, although its origins are not entirely clear. It is most often found on textiles and wallpapers, especially those requiring a large-scale pattern using only two colours or textures, such as cut velvets, damasks and flocks.

WALLPAPER
British, probably about 1913
Designed by Sydney Vacher
Colour machine print
E.2195–1913
The pomegranate pattern has been a traditional favourite for wall coverings and textiles ever since its introduction in the fifteenth century, usually on a large scale and with simple colourways.

THE ANNUNCIATION
Spanish, about 1527
By Pedro Romana of Córdoba
Oil on canvas on panel
D2 (Dyce Bequest, 1869)

Behind the Virgin Mary's head is a panel of silk woven with the pomegranate pattern. This may have symbolic overtones, since within the Christian tradition the pomegranate, with its seeds enclosed within the fruit, is an emblem of chastity.

Confusingly, the same seeds make it a symbol of fertility in oriental and classical decoration. The painting was originally a side panel from an altarpiece.

VELVET
*Italian, about
1450–1500
Silk velvet
1123–1888*
One reason for the success of the pomegranate pattern may have been that designs like this, on a relatively large scale, were best suited to show off velvet techniques.

Plant patterns:
naturalistic flowers

It is quite rare to find ornament with flowers or plants taken directly from nature: often stylized ones fit the purpose better. An exception occurred in the seventeenth century, when a growing general and scientific interest in plants and gardening was echoed in decoration. Lushly realistic flowers such as roses, tulips, lilies and crown imperials bloomed in still-life paintings, and on enamels, marquetry, textiles and almost every other medium. But imaginary and conventionalized plants also remained popular: vigorously scrolling acanthus (see pp.54–5) frequently provided a regular framework for designs.

After this, naturalistic flowers never fell entirely from favour: botanical engravings were an important source for silks and ceramics in the mid-eighteenth century, for instance. A rather overwhelmingly luxuriant version of naturalism appeared in the 1840s: the hot-house abundance of the ornament at the Great Exhibition in 1851 repelled many of the judges. Over the next fifty years many deliberate attempts were made to reinterpret and simplify floral patterns.

SILK PANEL FROM A DRESS
British, about 1745
Made in Spitalfields, London
Brocaded silk on a satin ground
T.104a–1986 (Given by Mrs Zoe Read in memory
of her parents, Ferdinand M.G. Bonnaud, ARCA,
and Hilda Bonnaud)
Posies of recognizable and realistically coloured flowers are scattered on the plain background of this silk. The naturalistic silk designs of the mid-eighteenth century owed a good deal to contemporary botanical engravings.

DISH
English, 1670–85
Made in London
Tin-glazed earthenware, painted
C.895–1935 (Given by Professor F.H. Garner)
Tulips and carnations are not native to Europe, but were introduced from Turkey and the Near East. The decoration on this charger also derives from Turkish designs and from Iznik ceramics of the sixteenth century, but the design and colouring are much bolder and coarser.

COVERED VASE
British, about 1840
Possibly made in the Minton factory
Porcelain, painted in enamel colours and gilt,
encrusted with flowers and leaves in high relief
C.20&a–1975
This is an example of the overloaded naturalism of the mid-nineteenth century that so appalled the judges at the Great Exhibition of 1851.

EDGING PAPER FOR SHELVES
Spanish, about 1950
Probably made in Barcelona or Valencia
Colour offset
E.962–1976 (Given by Signor Isidre Vallés)
A twentieth-century version of naturalism, showing modern hybrid tea roses.

Natural patterning

Many of the raw materials we use to make things are already ornamented. Wood and marble and animal skins, for instance, can all be finished in ways that show off their natural markings. These patterns can also be imitated on other materials, to make cheaper copies or just as a decorative finish. Nature has provided us with many other irregular or abstract patterns, from the clouds in the sky to the tracks left in the ground by worms.

This type of ornament has been widely used without being much affected by changes in fashion. Sometimes, science will add new patterns to the repertory, such as those of crystal structures.

DISH
Hungarian,
c.1680–1700
Tin-glazed earthenware
207–1906 (Given by Lt.
Col. G.B. Croft-Lyons)
The colours on this dish have been splashed on to create an effect vaguely reminiscent of marble, but adapted from the *bleu persan* decoration used on Nevers faience at this date.

PAIR OF LADIES' SHOES
British, about 1928
Natural snakeskin, lined with light tan leather and canvas, and with a white metal buckle.
T.308&a–1970
The natural pattern of the snake's skin is used to decorate these shoes.

TEAPOT
British, about 1807–13
Made by Barr, Flight and Barr of Worcester
Porcelain, painted and gilt
C.27&a–1964
The wriggling ground pattern is known as vermiculation and is intended to imitate worm tracks (from the Latin *vermiculatus*, full of worms). It was originally used as a finish on ancient Roman stone architecture and spread to ceramics and textiles in the eighteenth century.

PANEL: 'HAEMOGLOBIN'

British, about 1951
Designed by Martin Rowland
Made by Warerite Ltd
Laminated plastic (Warerite)
Circ.45–1968

Crystallography provided the starting point for the 26 manufacturers of the Festival Pattern Group involved in the Festival of Britain of 1951. Dr Helen Megaw's diagrams of the crystal structures of substances like boric acid, insulin, aluminium hydroxide and haemoglobin were used to create designs for ceramics, textiles, wallpapers and other products.

below

BOOKBINDERS' MARBLED PAPERS

British, about 1897
Paper and ink
E.6326.14, 25, 44, 55, 67 & 83–1897

Marbled papers were introduced into Europe from the Near East about 1600. They are produced by suspending colours on a liquid surface, manipulating them into patterns (either physically or with the help of chemicals) and absorbing them onto paper.

ARCHITECTURAL ORNAMENT: THE CLASSICAL ORDERS

The orders (from the Italian *ordine*: rule, class or arrangement) were the basis of ancient Greek and Roman architecture. From about 1500 until recent times their structure, proportions and decoration have dominated European and American architecture and design. Each order consists of a column headed by a capital, supporting a beam, or entablature, which is divided into an architrave, frieze and cornice. About 2,600 years ago the Greek Doric and Ionic orders were developed from wooden columns into a regularized system for building in stone, with standard components, proportions and ornament. They were later joined by Corinthian, the Romans adding Tuscan (a form of Doric) and Composite. The system of orders was classified by the ancient Roman architect Vitruvius (who excluded Composite) in the *Ten Books of Architecture*, but in reality the ancient architects used the orders very freely; not until the 1400s were the five orders regarded as a set, representing the most perfect form of architecture. Ranged in order of size and elaboration, each order had a particular personality and symbolic meaning, its proportions related to those of the human figure. Many architects have tried to devise the ideal, perfectly proportioned set, adaptable to all parts of a building.

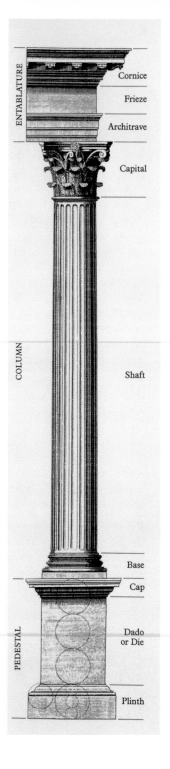

opposite, above left

MODEL OF A TOMB AT PALMYRA, SYRIA
French, 1821
Made by Jean-Pierre Fouquet of Paris
Plaster of Paris with metal armature
Circ.217–1916

The choice of a classical order sets the character of the building to which it is applied. For the fronts of temples and other religious buildings in antiquity, porticoes made up of columns decorated the front and back, topped by the flat triangular shape known as the pediment. Architects since antiquity have studied important classical prototypes for their own designs. This tomb in the shape of a temple is one of a series of models of Greek and Roman architecture ordered in Paris about 1820 by the architect John Nash for display in his Gallery of Architecture at 14–16 Regent Street in London. Visitors were clearly meant to reflect upon the influence of the great buildings of the past on Nash's own improvements to the urban fabric of London. The main source for this model was Robert Wood's illustration in *The Ruins of Palmyra*, published in 1753.

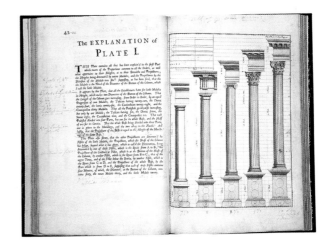

 below

TUTTE L'OPERE D'ARCHITETTURA ET PROSPETTIVA
About 1619
By Sebastiano Serlio
Published in Vicenza by Giacomo de Franceschi
86 S 23

Serlio's account of the orders, first published in 1537, was the earliest to present them as a complete and authoritative series. His pioneering woodcut illustration shows, from left to right, the standard set: Tuscan, Doric, Ionic, Corinthian and Composite. Serlio's books made him the most important architectural writer of the sixteenth century. This volume belonged in the seventeenth century to the Bishop of Chartres and Reims, and in the nineteenth century to the architect Joseph Gwilt.

A TREATISE OF THE FIVE ORDERS OF
COLUMNS IN ARCHITECTURE
1708
By Claude Perrault, translated by John James
Published in London by Benjamin Motte. First
published in Paris in 1676
62 B 17

Attempts to produce the perfect set of orders culminated in the work of French academicians like Perrault, who was designing the Louvre in Paris when this work was first published. Ever since Vitruvius, the orders have been measured by column diameters, generally divided into two modules, themselves divided into minutes. This plate was designed to demonstrate the general rule of mathematical progression, each column in turn rising by the distance of one column diameter. As they rise the columns become lighter and more decorated. John Sturt's illustrations here faithfully copy the original French engravings. The book has been annotated, and criticized, by an eighteenth-century reader.

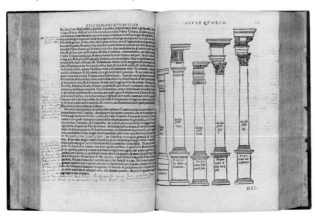

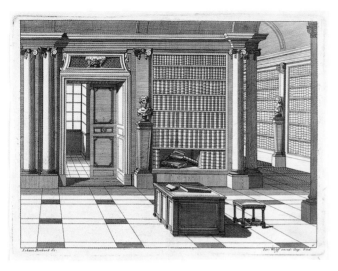

TWO DESIGNS FOR INTERIORS
German, about 1705
By Johann Boxbart, copied from Desseins de differents Lambris *of about 1675 by G. Feuillet.*
Published by Jeremias Wolff in Augsburg
Engravings
E.2471&3–1913
The use of the classical orders here determines the scale of the interior architecture, whether as fully architectural, supporting columns, or as flat pilasters carrying through two 'storeys' of panelling above a base and dado. The same scale divisions, but without visible orders, are still used in interiors today.

The Doric order

The Doric order is named after the Dorian peoples, who lived in mainland Greece and the western Greek colonies. The first stone examples of its use date from 550 BC, but its features echo the functional parts of wooden architecture, especially the mutules, triglyphs and guttae of the frieze and entablature. The simplicity of Doric encouraged the use of subtle refinements to correct optical distortions. Greek Doric columns have no base. The Roman Doric order, which added a base and decorated the capital, was taken up by Renaissance architects; the Greek type was not revived until about 1760. The Roman architect Vitruvius, who compared the proportions of Doric with those of a 'well-built male', recommended it for temples to virile gods. Similar ideas have suggested its use on civic and military buildings. Tuscan was used by the Etruscans in Italy and resembles a simplified Doric. Taken up by the Romans, it was systematized into an order by Renaissance scholars.

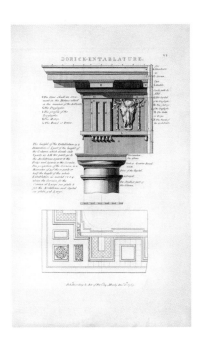

DORICK ENTABLATURE

British, 1769
By Matthias Darly from The
Ornamental Architect, *1771*
Engraving
E.2217–1908

Darly here shows a simple un-
fluted Roman Doric – the 'ovolo or
quarter round' of the capital is now
usually called the echinus. The
hanging pegs are mutules, the
upright grooved block the triglyph.
Darly was a self-styled 'Professor
of Ornament' and an engraver. His
aim in this and other prints of The
Ornamental Architect was to
disseminate them to artists of all
kinds, strongly emphasizing their
ornamental aspect. His illustrations
are based on James Gibbs's Rules
for Drawing the Several Parts of
Architecture (1732).

left

THE GREEK DORIC ORDER

British, about 1769
Engraved by Thomas Miller after Nicholas
Revett
Engraving
29481.58

The much simpler form of the Greek Doric
capital is shown with an undecorated echinus
finishing in a set of bands. The flutings of
Greek Doric columns normally have no flat
moulding between them. This print is from
Volume 1 of *Ionian Antiquities* (1769),
published by the Society of Dilettanti, one of
the earliest works to make surveys of real
Greek buildings. It shows a capital, entablature
and cornice found near the temple of Athene
Polias at Priene (about 334 BC).

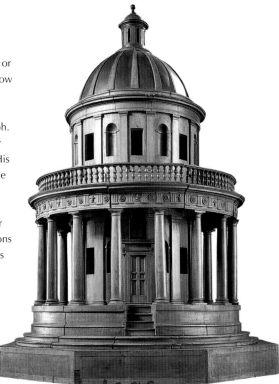

MODEL, BASED ON BRAMANTE'S TEMPIETTO

19th century
Walnut and pearwood
A.5–1987 (Given by Mrs Denis Roberts)

Commissioned in 1502 by King Ferdinand and Queen Isabella of Spain, the
Tempietto marks the spot on the Janiculum Hill in Rome where St Peter was
supposedly martyred. It was built by the architect Donato Bramante and was
probably completed by 1512. Just as the antique writer on architecture, Vitruvius,
advised the use of the Doric order for temples dedicated to important male gods,
so Bramante used the Roman version of the order for the chief male saint of the
Christian Church. The building became an important example of the use of Doric
from the High Renaissance, and was much illustrated and discussed in books of
architectural theory.

The Ionic order

The Ionic order is named after the Ionian peoples, Greeks living on the eastern Aegean islands and the coast of Asia Minor (which is now in Turkey). It originated there about 2,600 years ago, but took longer to standardize than the Doric order and has always been freer and more flexible. It has two possible types of main beam or entablature, which originated in different places. One uses bracket-like modillions and a frieze; the other features dentils, or a series of small blocks, which probably imitate the crossbeams of its wooden ancestor, and was originally without a frieze. The capital, with its curling volutes, has different Greek, Roman and 'modern' variants, and there are several different types of column base. Ionic is taller in its proportions than Doric, and according to Vitruvius had 'feminine slenderness'. Its calm refinement was thought to make it suitable for temples dedicated to such deities as Diana and Apollo, and buildings connected with the arts and learning.

IONIC CAPITAL FROM AN ATTACHED COLUMN
British, late 18th century
Wood
W.29–1990
This is a simplified version of a capital designed about 1765 by Robert Adam for Syon House. The heavy curving cushion-like voluted section of this capital is characteristic of Greek Ionic, and in this example has been copied (with the plaited band and moulding below) from the Erectheum in Athens. Adam has added acanthus leaves and rosettes from a 'modern' Ionic capital. Greek Ionic was not usually copied in its pure form until about 1800.

ENTABLATURE
British, 1991
Plaster
A.8–2005
This type of capital, with its straight moulding between the volutes, appeared towards the end of the Greek development and was taken up by the Romans and Renaissance architects. This entablature has dentils, which originated in Asia Minor, and a frieze. This type of Ionic is based on that published by Vignola in 1562.

IONIC CAPITALS
British, 1770
By Matthias Darly, from The Ornamental Architect, *1771*
Engraving
E.2233–1908
This type of Ionic capital, with two short curling volutes, is known as 'modern'. It had in fact appeared in ancient Rome and looks very like the upper Ionic part of the Composite capital.

The Corinthian order

The Corinthian order is named after the Greek city of Corinth, but its origin is obscure. According to legend, the bronze-worker Callimachus was inspired to create it by the sight of a basket through which an acanthus plant had grown. Interestingly, Corinth was famous for its bronzes and the thin open forms of the capital do suggest an origin in metalwork. The capital appeared occasionally in Greek temple interiors from the late fifth century BC onwards, but in combination with the entablature and base of the Ionic order. The Romans made it their chief architectural order for public buildings, enriching it by adding brackets, or modillions, to the cornice and loading the entablature with decorated mouldings. Its leading position was revived in the Renaissance, perhaps because of its great richness and the adaptability of its forms and ornament. In proportion the Corinthian is taller than the Ionic, and according to Vitruvius recalled 'the slight figure of a young girl'.

I QUATTRO LIBRI DELL'ARCHITETTURA
1570
By Andrea Palladio
Published in Venice by Domenico de' Franceschi, 1570
87 B 51

Palladio's illustration shows a version of the Corinthian order in the Forum of Nerva (or the Transitorium) in Rome, dedicated in AD 97. He illustrates several other parts of the buildings as well as the bases, capitals and entablatures. The Corinthian capital is formed from an inverted bell-shape surrounded by two rows of acanthus leaves, out of which spring curling stems or cauliculi. Like other types of acanthus, it was compared with a real leaf (of an olive tree), but in fact the whole composition is very like the imaginary leaf-and-scroll motifs first devised in fifth-century BC Greece. Palladio's woodcuts were the first large collection of accurate illustrations of ancient Roman architecture.

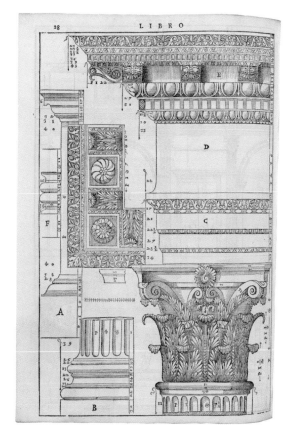

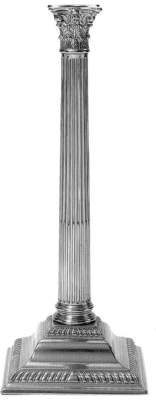

CANDLESTICK
British, about 1770
Nickel-brass (tutenag)
M.674–1926 (Croft-Lyons Bequest)
Column-shaped candlesticks may have been inspired by freestanding columns in Rome; they also formed part of the symbolic regalia of Freemasons. The filling in of the lower parts of the flutes in this example is known as cabling.

*A PARALLEL OF THE
ANCIENT
ARCHITECTURE WITH
THE MODERN*
1723
*By Roland Fréart de Chambray,
translated by John Evelyn
Published in London by D.
Brown and others; first English
edition 1664; originally
published in Paris in 1650*
33 G 1

The illustration shows
Vitruvius's story of the
discovery of the Corinthian
order. A virgin of Corinth fell
sick and died. Her nurse
placed a basket of vessels and
other funeral things on her
grave, putting a tile on top to
keep it dry. The basket had
been placed on an acanthus
root, which grew to envelop it,
and inspired Callimachus to
design the capital.

Fréart's *Parallel* was the
earliest critical comparison of
ancient and modern versions of
the orders. It was 'made
English for the benefit of
builders' by John Evelyn, with
the aim of preventing 'busie
and Gothick triflings in the
composition of the Five
Orders'.

The Composite order and irregular inventions

The Composite order has a capital that combines the volutes of the Ionic with the acanthus leaves of the Corinthian, and a base and entablature closely related to those of the Corinthian. It was a Roman invention of about AD 50, and may have had a special patriotic significance. It was only raised to the status of an order by Renaissance scholars, who observed it in ancient buildings. Its name was coined by Sebastiano Serlio. The Composite was but one of a large number of Roman and Hellenistic capital types that played variations on the theme of the Corinthian and other regular orders. Since the 1400s, these irregular treatments have inspired many new inventions, ranging from the new 'national' orders, such as Philibert de L'Orme's French order of 1567, to the 'Fancy Capitals' of Matthias Darly shown here.

THE COMPOSITE ORDER
Italian, 1635
From Giacomo Barozzi da Vignola's Regola delli Cinque Ordini d'Architettura, *first published 1562*
Engraving
62 C 53
Vignola's book on the five orders, based on Roman examples, was a set of engravings without a text. In spite of this it had an immense influence, being reissued in ever-expanding editions right up to the nineteenth century.

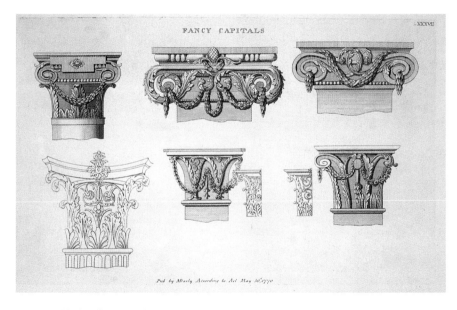

FANCY CAPITALS
British, 1770
By Matthias Darly, from The Ornamental Architect, *1771*
Engraving
E.2248–1908
'Fancy' now means elaborately decorated; in Darly's time it meant imaginative or inventive. Here he plays variations on the Ionic, Corinthian and Composite capitals. They are characteristic of the Neo-classical style.

ARCHITECTURAL ORNAMENT: CLASSICAL DECORATION

Just as the architectural systems of the Greek and Roman orders are all around us, so their ornaments can still be found on buildings, interiors and everyday objects. Most common are their mouldings, either simply shaped (p.46) or enriched (pp.48–53). In addition to this repeating ornament there are single motifs that can be used in many different ways, notably leaf forms developed from the acanthus plant (pp.54–5) that has dominated European ornament for 2,000 years. The floral palmette (pp.56–7), like many Greek motifs, was borrowed and developed from ancient Egyptian and Near Eastern forms. It had a long subsequent history in India and the Far East and in Islamic ornament. Other single motifs represent actual objects used by the Greeks and Romans and originally had religious or symbolic significance. Some, such as the trophy (pp.62–3), have retained their meaning; others, like the little sacrificial dish or patera (p.58), have become purely ornamental.

Mouldings

The shaped parts of the classical orders are called mouldings. Their forms were designed to throw off rainwater and to give a decorative and satisfying sequence of light and shade when seen together. The mouldings of the ancient Greeks and Romans are still all around us: on our buildings, in our interiors and on everyday things – from picture frames to coffee pots. They still perform the same function as they did in ancient times: decorating and shaping something that is essentially practical. The names of the mouldings reveal their Greek and Roman ancestry, as well as the work of Renaissance scholars. Some of them have also passed down to the language of today's building and carpentry trades. The more elaborate orders have inspired a huge number of added enrichments, which further developed the forms shown here.

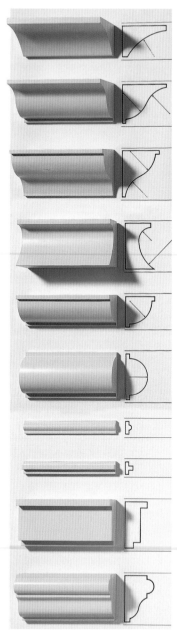

PLAIN MOULDINGS (from top)
Cavetto. From Italian: little hollow
Cyma recta. From Greek and Latin: upright wave
Cyma reversa. From Greek and Latin: wave turned backwards. Also called ogee
Scotia. From Greek: darkness (referring to the shadow)
Ovolo. From Italian: egg, after its typical use in egg and dart decoration. Also called echinus (Greek) and quarter-round

Torus. From Latin: a swelling or knot
Astragal. From Greek: a huckle-bone, the ball joint of the ankle. Also a called a cock-bead
Fillet. From Latin: a little thread. Also called a listel
Fascia. From Latin: a band
Bolection. Derivation unknown. This moulding, which was not used in ancient times, joins two surfaces at different levels. This example is made up of a cyma recta, a torus and fillets

PORTRAIT OF A WOMAN IN AN OVAL FRAME
Low Countries, 1631; the frame British, early 18th century
By an anonymous artist
Inscribed 'Aetatis Suae [her age] 23/1631'
Oil on copper; the frame gilt and ebonized fruitwood
P.104–1931 (Gift of W.A.J. Floersheim)

Frames, especially those for pictures, draw attention to an object as well as protecting it. On this frame the plain outer mouldings contrast with the narrower but richly decorated inner moulding. It leads our eye towards the picture and emphasizes its value as an object. The painting belonged to Sir Robert Walpole, who probably had the frame made. It passed to his son Horace Walpole, who described it as a portrait of the wife of the painter Cornelis van Poelenburgh, 'by him'.

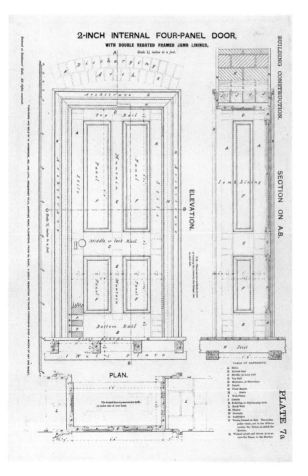

TWO-INCH INTERNAL FOUR-PANEL DOOR
British, about 1860
Published and sold by W. Busbridge, Plumstead
Lithograph
540C

This diagram for builders (which cost 3d a sheet) shows how the forms and proportions of classical mouldings were used in ordinary rooms in the nineteenth and early twentieth centuries. The moulding surrounding the door is called an architrave, and does indeed resemble that part of the classical orders.

CHOCOLATE POT
British, London hallmarks for 1722–3; sponsor's mark illegible
Engraved with the arms of Willis
Silver
M.379–1927 (Given by Major A.J. Carter, DSO, and his wife)

As in the classical orders, the undecorated areas in this coffee pot are divided up by carefully placed mouldings. They play a vital role in hiding and strengthening joins and edges.

Enriched mouldings 1

The mouldings used on the classical orders are frequently decorated, or 'enriched'. Some enrichments are related to mouldings of a particular shape and most first appeared in connection with certain orders. Away from their strictly architectural setting, enriched mouldings have developed into a huge number of types. The Vitruvian scroll (or wave scroll) is named after the Roman architect Vitruvius, but is actually far older in origin, having emerged in Egypt some 3,500 years ago. It is used chiefly on flat surfaces, in many variations. The complex interlacing bands of the guilloche were used on Greek temples about 600 BC, but had been invented some 1,000 years before in the Near East. Although often used on flat surfaces, the guilloche is also used on torus mouldings (see p.46). Rope-like cable moulding was also used on the torus, or the smaller astragal.

below
PANEL WITH GUILLOCHE DECORATION
English, about 1625
Oak
457–1898
In the eighteenth century this type of guilloche was called 'twisted ribbon and flower'. The panel is probably from a piece of furniture or a set of wall panelling.

right below
MOULD FOR COMPOSITION ORNAMENT: VITRUVIAN SCROLL
British, about 1820
Boxwood
W.62–1989 (Given by Clark & Fenn Ltd, incorporating G. Jackson & Sons Ltd)
Except for the leaves between the scrolls, this design is similar to the earliest type of Vitruvian scroll. It is also known as wave scroll and running dog. This mould is for making ornament for application to furniture and interior fixtures, such as chimneypieces.

CONCORDE CUP AND SAUCER
British, about 1984
Designed by Malcolm Keen
Made by Steelite International for Royal Doulton
Bone china with high-temperature colours and gilding.
C94&a–1984 (Given by Royal Doulton)
A row of Concorde airliners, their noses drooping, forms a version of the Vitruvian scroll around the rim.

DESSERT BASKET WITH VITRUVIAN SCROLL ORNAMENT
German, about 1780
Modelled by Michel-Victor Acier for the Meissen factory
Porcelain
C.303–1921 (Given by Mr C.H. Campbell)
The basket also has ram's head and festoon decoration.

SALVER WITH A ROPEWORK BORDER
English, London hallmarks for 1694–5
Mark IR with two fleurs-de-lis above and one below, over-striking another mark
Silver
M.40–1967 (Given by Miss D. Stockwell)
Ropework was a favourite ornament of the seventeenth century, when the bulging forms of gadrooning were also popular. Here the relief ornament strengthens the thin metal, like the corrugations in a plastic cup.

DISH DECORATED WITH GUILLOCHES
French, 1550–1600
Made by Bernard Pallisy or a follower
Earthenware painted in enamel colours
5961–1859

Enriched mouldings 2

Most of the enriched moulding shown here first appeared on the Ionic order and came to be used on Corinthian and Composite as well. The descriptively named egg and dart, the chief ornament for the ovolo moulding, was formed by removing the palmettes from a lotus and palmette strip (see p.56) and replacing them with rounded 'eggs'. The similar waterleaf is mostly used on the cyma reversa (see p.46). Bead and reel can be used to accentuate an astragal, together with necklace-like beading in many varieties. The Greek key pattern was devised in ancient Egypt, as was the Vitruvian scroll. Together with the guilloche they are the main classical decoration for flat mouldings and borders. Fluting was used to ornament columns; as a Greek border ornament (especially on flat surfaces) it may have derived from Egypt or the Near East.

above

WALLPAPER BORDER: EGG AND DART

British, about 1830–40
From the stock of Cowtan & Sons (successors to J. Duppa, J.G. Grace and several other firms)
Colour print from wood blocks
E.56–1939 (Given by Mr A.C. Cowtan in memory of his father, Arthur Barnard Cowtan, OBE)
Egg and dart is often accompanied by bead and reel. It is also known as egg and anchor. 'Egg and tongue' lacks the arrowhead-like element. At the bottom of this border is a line of bead and reel.

below

WALLPAPER BORDER: WATERLEAF AND TONGUE

British, about 1840–50
Colour print from wood blocks
E.1764–1934
This border is from the logbook of Arthur Sanderson & Sons, where it is described as 'Archer's cornice'. It imitates the decoration on the cyma reversa moulding on Greek Ionic cornices, for instance of the Erectheum in Athens. At its base is a strip of bead and reel.

JUG WITH BEADED DECORATION

British, late 18th century
Sheffield plate
M.335–1912
This jug is decorated only with beaded decoration borders and waterleaves on the cover.

right

SAMPLE BOARD OF BEADING, BEAD AND REEL AND ROPE WORK ORNAMENT

British, early 20th century
Composition on wood
Weald and Downland Museum loan
This board was used by a manufacturer of composition ornament.

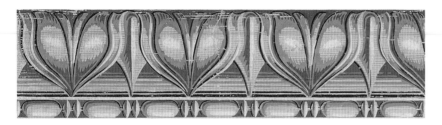

STORAGE JAR (AMPHORA) DECORATED WITH GREEK KEY

Greek, about 520–500 BC
Made in Athens
Found in an Etruscan tomb at Vulci in Italy
Earthenware decorated in the black-figure technique
4796–1901

The strip below the figures is the simplest kind of Greek key – it can turn into a complicated interlace pattern. On the neck of the vase is an early type of lotus and palmette pattern (see p.56), the origin of egg and dart. The Greek key is also known as fret, and meander. The figure scene shows Athena between Herakles (Hercules) and Iolaos.

EGGCUPS WITH PIERCED FLUTING IN A STAND

British, 1780–1800
Sheffield plate
Circ.399–1925

The frame is decorated with reeding. This imaginative yet simple use of classical motifs is typical of British Neo-classical metalwork, designed to be made with the help of machines.

CASTING MODEL FOR FLUTED ORNAMENT

British, early 20th century
Made by George Jackson & Sons
Soft wood
W.858–1989 (Given by Clark & Fenn Ltd, incorporating G. Jackson & Sons Ltd)

This is a positive model for making a flexible mould for composition ornament. The husks filling the flutes are called cabling.

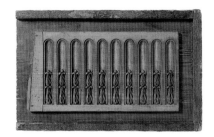

Plant ornament: enriched mouldings

Plants have inspired many different ways of decorating architectural mouldings, but the ancient Greeks got little further than the lotus and palmette strip (see pp.56–7). The Romans, however, developed a wide variety of rich leaf mouldings to accompany the acanthus of Corinthian and Composite capitals (see pp.43–5). Baroque architects of the later 1600s developed the Roman types into a large number of different forms, which fully exploited the twisting and turning of the leaves. Trailing plant ornament used as a flat strip was a Greek ornamental invention. Plants such as the vine, ivy and oak often related to particular gods and had symbolic meanings, but were also used as pure decoration. Since ancient times other plants have been used in the same symbolic or decorative way.

below
MOULDING ENRICHED
WITH ACANTHUS
English, about 1670
Oak
W.860–1989 (Given by Clark &
Fenn Ltd, incorporating G. Jackson
& Sons Ltd)
This was a favourite type of Baroque moulding, used here on a cyma recta. Such carved decoration was often left unpainted.

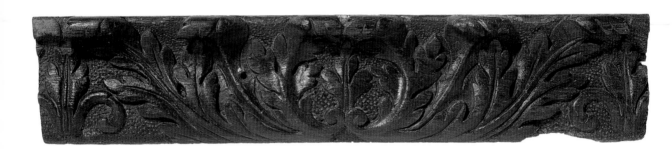

PLATE WITH OAK-LEAF BORDER
French, 1808–18
Made in the Creil factory, printed by
Stone, Cocquerel and Le Gros of Paris
Cream-coloured earthenware with transfer
printing
C.324–1912 (Given by Lt. Col. Dingwall,
DSO, through the National Art Collections
Fund)
In ancient times the oak was sacred to
Zeus (Jupiter), the god of thunder. Since
the late eighteenth century plant trails
have been especially popular on
ceramics.

left below

ARCHITRAVE WITH ACANTHUS DECORATION
British, about 1760
From Pembroke House, Whitehall
Pine, originally painted
Circ.88–1913
The acanthus-leaf ornament here
carved on cyma recta mouldings
(with bead and reel in-between) is
one of many variations using three-
lobed framing elements. In French
it is called *trefles* (trefoils) *et
fleurons*. This door surround
closely imitates a single fascia from
an architrave of the Corinthian and
Composite orders.

JUG DECORATED WITH HOPS
British, dated
21 January 1806
Made by Barr, Flight and
Barr of Worcester
Porcelain with gilded
decoration
Circ.539–1910
The hop border on the
neck indicates that this
jug is for beer.

Plant ornament: the acanthus

The ornament known as acanthus, named after a common Mediterranean plant, first appeared in Greece about 2,500 years ago. Although the leaves of Greek acanthus ornament are like the real *acanthus spinosus* plant, they were from the start linked to the palmette (see p.56) and quickly developed into a living but imaginary plant, with curling stems and palmette 'flowers'. The leaves also became part of the Corinthian capital (see p.43). The very rich scrolling type of acanthus developed by the Romans gave to European ornament an extremely adaptable leaf form, which has been in use ever since and has inspired similar decorative treatments of other plants. It became the leading decorative element in the Baroque style of the seventeenth century, especially in Northern Europe, and a standard drawing exercise for apprentice craftsmen. Although usually purely ornamental, the acanthus may have originated as a symbol of death.

PLATE, PAINTED WITH
ACANTHUS SPINOSUS
British, about 1760
Made by the Chelsea factory
Porcelain, painted
C.58–1948
The plant is copied from an illustration in Philip Miller's *Figures of Plants* (1750)

STORAGE JAR (*PELIKE*)
Italian, about 370–360 BC
Made in Apulia
Earthenware decorated in the red-figure technique
C.2493–1910 (Salting Collection)
This jar was made in a part of southern Italy that was under Greek influence, about 100 years after the invention of acanthus ornament. The acanthus leaves at the base of the pot are in their early naturalistic form, but imaginary scrolling stems and flowers spring from them. The figure scene shows Dionysus and Ariadne embracing, flanked by two women, with Eros above. On the other side is another figure scene.

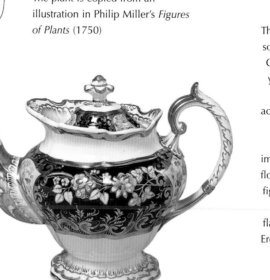

TEAPOT
British, about 1830
Spode factory
Porcelain
553c–1902
All the curling and leaf ornament on this teapot is inspired by the acanthus.

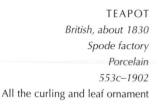

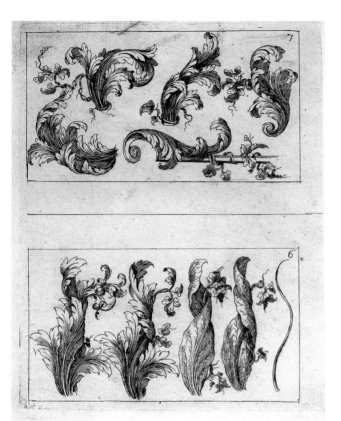

PRINTS SHOWING HOW TO DRAW AN ACANTHUS LEAF
French, 1713
By E. Roberday, from Livres de principes de l'ornement, *plates 6 and 7*
Etching
29833.3
Drawing the acanthus was an essential skill for seventeenth- and eighteenth-century designers and craftsmen. By going back to the principles of growth seen in nature, Roberday gives life to the increasingly complicated imaginary leaf.

AN ANCIENT ROMAN CARVING IN THE CHURCH OF SAN SILVESTRO, ROME
Italian, about 1525–50
Perhaps engraved by Agostino Veneziano, published by Antonio Salamanca
Engraving
16796
The ancient Roman scrolling acanthus was recorded by Renaissance artists, who also took over its population of animals and insects. Although it was actually highly artificial, the Romans believed that their acanthus represented the local Italian *acanthus mollis*; ever since that time people have tried to classify different types of acanthus ornament by linking them to specific plants.

PORRIDGE TUB
Norwegian, about 1800
Made in Gulbrandsdal
Carved and painted wood
594–1891
Densely curling acanthus was a chief element in the Baroque style from about 1650. It did not reach Norway until about 1700, and became part of folk art, in which it continues to this day. The paint on this tub was added later in the nineteenth century.

Plant ornament:
the palmette and anthemion

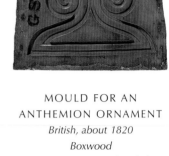

The palmette was invented in Egypt about 3,500 years ago. Although it is now named after the palm-tree, the palmette probably represented an imaginary flower. It had a huge influence in Europe and reached as far as China, where it inspired the peony motif. In Egypt it was often shown hanging down in a band, alternating with the sacred lotus flower. In the Near East the Egyptian band was turned the other way up, emphasizing the palmette. Taken up by the Greeks from about 600 BC, the lotus and palmette band became a standard European edge pattern, for flat surfaces and cyma mouldings (see p.46). The Greeks also developed a complete imaginary plant, formed from scrolling lines with attached palmettes and acanthus leaves (see p.54). The more flower-like palmette of the Greeks is called the anthemion (Greek, *anthos*: flower). The palmette is also used on its own, especially as a decoration for the roofs of buildings.

MOULD FOR AN
ANTHEMION ORNAMENT
British, about 1820
Boxwood
W.617–1989 (Given by Clark &
Fenn Ltd, incorporating G. Jackson
& Sons Ltd)
In composition this mould for the manufacture of relief ornament is based on a Greek architectural gable finial or acroter.

TOP SECTION OF A MIRROR FRAME
British, late 18th century
Carved wood with composition, painted blue (originally a darker shade) and gilded.
691–1891
In this Neo-classical design the palmettes have become inverted shells and the lotus flowers have turned into leaf sprays. The waving band that connects them, which was devised in ancient Greece, is the basis of all other plant ornament based on the waving band.

VASE
Italian, about 1480
Probably made in Pesaro
Tin-glazed earthenware (maiolica)
8529–1863
This vase shows a favourite version of the palmette and lotus strip, in which the flowers oppose each other. The ornament is probably derived from an ancient Roman carving.

DRINKING CUP
Greek, about 520 BC
Made in Athens
Earthenware, decorated in the red-figure technique.
275–1864
While scrolling line ornament had appeared all over the Mediterranean in early times, it was the Greeks who developed it into freely spreading patterns. Linked to palmettes and then acanthus leaves, they became universally useful imaginary plants. This cup, which recalls the work of painter called Psiax, is inscribed in Greek: 'Braxas is beautiful'.

INVITATION CARD
British, 1808
Printed by William Savage Bedford Bury,
Covent Garden
Engraving and letterpress
434b–1898
This invitation is to the laying of the foundation stone of the Theatre Royal in Covent Garden. The alternating palmettes and lotus flowers of ancient Egypt are clearly visible in the border, but the lotus has turned into little more than a frame for the palmettes. This border is probably copied from a print of a Greek vase.

AT THE **PIAZZA-DOOR** ONLY,
ADMIT THE BEARER
TO THE **LAYING** OF THE
FOUNDATION-STONE
OF
THE **THEATRE ROYAL** IN
COVENT-GARDEN.
DEC. 31st, 1808.

No Carriages admitted into Bow-Street.

From objects into ornament 1

A number of well-known ornamental motifs began life as representations of objects used in the religious ceremonies of the Greeks and Romans and at first had a symbolic meaning. Leafy garlands (also called swags or festoons) were hung on sacrificial animals, as well as temples and altars, and also on sarcophagi. As ornament they are often employed with other symbols, including paterae, dishes used at sacrifices. As decoration, paterae can be round or oval. Overlapping paterae form the money pattern. Fruit, flowers, vegetables, husks and cloth (see p.63) are also used with garlands. Wreaths were originally leafy crowns given as a sign of honour; they are still used on prizes, memorials and uniforms. The rosette, a basic flower motif, emerged in ancient Egypt and was later taken up in Greece.

GARLANDS
Dutch, 1665–9
By Hubertus Quellien after Artus Quellien
Etching
24875.11
Heavy and richly decorated garlands were characteristic of Baroque ornament. Artus Quellien's pioneering ornaments at Amsterdam Town Hall include these marble garlands in the gallery, carved in the 1650s. They symbolize (from the top) Venus, Apollo, Jupiter and Mars.

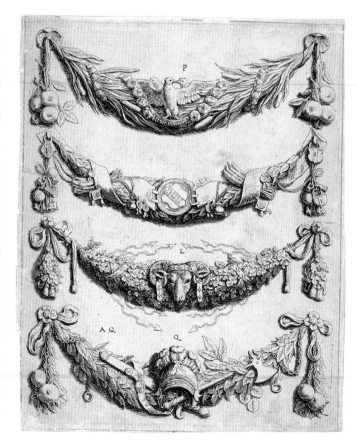

THREE MOULDS FOR PATERAE
British, about 1820
Hardwood
W.716–1989, 771–1989, & 786–1989 (Given by Clark and Fenn Ltd, incorporating G. Jackson & Sons Ltd)
The huge range of these useful motifs is shown in this group. These moulds are for composition ornament, to be applied to furniture or interiors.

PLATE DECORATED WITH HUSK GARLANDS

British, about 1775
Made in Staffordshire or Yorkshire
Cream-coloured earthenware painted in
green and black
C.70–1940

Husks, or open seedpods, were joined
together to form garlands: they are very
frequent in Neo-classical decoration. On this
plate the husk garlands are charmingly
irregular, and accompanied by naturalistic
flowers.

SAUCER WITH A GARLAND BORDER

French, dated 1812
Made in the Sèvres factory
Porcelain, painted in green and brown and gilded
C.26–1915 (Given by Lt. Col. K. Dingwall, DSO)

Thick laurel garlands are made to 'hang' around the
edge of the plate. Next comes a laurel or olive crown
or wreath and finally a rosette in the centre. In ancient
Greece crowns were made of bay (European laurel) or
olive leaves (or golden imitations of them). The
Romans added crowns of oak and woven grass. Heroic
wreaths and garland decorations were much used by
both sides during the Napoleonic wars.

From objects into ornament 2

The motifs shown here represent real objects used by the ancient Greeks and Romans. As ornament they can be purely decorative or have symbolic meaning. The tripod, a three-legged stand, became a characteristic motif of the Neo-classical style in the eighteenth century. The lyre was in legend given to Apollo, the Greek god of music and poetry. As a motif it is still linked to music and the arts. The flaming torch was the Greek symbol of life. Extinguished, it indicates death, especially on Christian monuments. Fasces (Latin: bundles) were the symbols of ancient Roman magistrates. Made of axes surrounded by wooden rods, they demonstrated the authority to punish. They still decorate civic and legal buildings. The cornucopia (Latin: horn of plenty), a goat's horn overflowing with fruits of the earth, was devised as a symbol of plenty and fertility and as such remains popular today.

TORCH
British, 20th century
Softwood, painted
W.855–1989
(Given by Clark & Fern Ltd, incorporating G. Jackson & Sons Ltd)
This decorative torch imitates an early nineteenth-century example. It was probably used as a casting model by George Jackson & Sons.

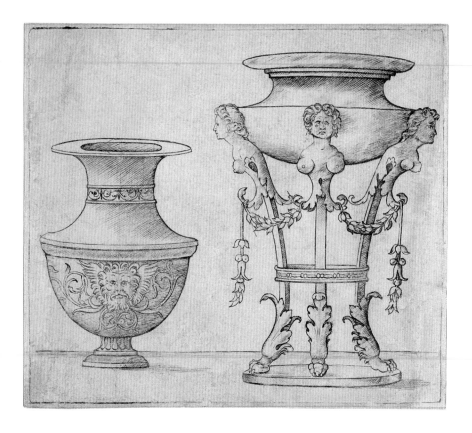

A VASE AND A TRIPOD
Italian, about 1515
Possibly by Giovanni Antonio da Brescia
Engraving
E.2232–1922 (From the Paul Davidsohn Collection)
This is the first Renaissance print to show vessels in the classical style. The vase is like bronze examples of the time. The tripod is probably based on representations in Roman reliefs or wall decorations.

LYRE WALLPAPER FRIEZE

British, 1911
Designed by Walter Crane in 1910 and made by Jeffrey & Co.
Colour print from wood blocks
E.5134–1919

In Greek legend the lyre was invented by Hermes (Mercury), who stretched strings over the shell of a tortoise. This frieze, which shows an ancient lyre made of tortoiseshell and goats' horns, is from a set of wallpapers called 'classic'.

DISH DECORATED WITH CORNUCOPIAE

French, 1550–1600
Made by Bernard Palissy or a follower
Lead-glazed earthenware, with hand-modelled, press-moulded and cast decorations
C.2319–1910

In Greek myth, the horn came from Amalthea, the goat that had suckled the infant Zeus. Horns were a very ancient symbol of growth and fertility.

below

DE DUCIBUS ET COMITIBUS PROVINCIALIBUS GALLIAE

By Antonius Dadinus Altesera
Published in Toulouse by Arnaldum Colobrium, 1643
Gold-tooled calf binding
AL1714–1887

The fasces on the mid-seventeenth-century binding of this book were the personal badge of Cardinal Mazarin.

From objects into ornament 3

The trophy (Greek: *tropaion*) began as a display of the weapons and armour of defeated enemies, either hung on a tree or heaped up. It was turned by the Romans into a decorative symbol of military power. The idea of a collection of objects brought together as a symbol was extended to include trophies describing many other human activities, such as hunting and music-making, as well as more general ideas. Ribbons and festoons play an important part in many types of classical ornament, including the trophy. As motifs on their own, curtain-like festoons, cloth versions of the plant garland, are useful edging ornament, while ribbons can be made to fill any space decoratively.

SABRE DECORATED WITH TROPHIES
British, London hallmarks for 1804–5. The blade is Turkish
Made by Richard Teed and supplied by Gilbert of London.
Steel and silver gilt
1606–1871

The handle is in the shape of a lion swallowing a serpent (the British Lion swallowing evil), while the scabbard is decorated with trophies, foliage, Britannia and the Royal Arms. The trophies include fasces (see p.60) and a pelta, a crescent-shaped shield. The sword probably belonged to Charles, Earl of Whitworth, Colonel Commandant of the Holmsdale Infantry.

TROPHIES OF THE HUNT
French, 1773
Crayon manner etching by Gilles Demarteau after Jean-Baptiste Huet
28083.B.3

SILK PANEL FROM A DRESS: RIBBON PATTERN

French, 1760–70
Silk, brocaded with silk chenille
Circ.502–1962
The lace and leopard-skin ribbons on this silk show the free naturalism with which ribbon ornament was treated in the eighteenth century.

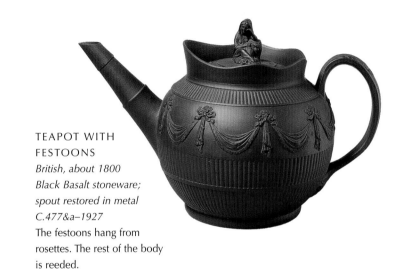

TEAPOT WITH FESTOONS

British, about 1800
Black Basalt stoneware;
spout restored in metal
C.477&a–1927
The festoons hang from rosettes. The rest of the body is reeded.

COTTON PRINTED WITH TROPHIES

French, early 19th century
Made in Jouy
Printed cotton ('Toiles de Jouy')
T.327–1919
The motifs include trophies of arms and artists' implements, cornucopiae, winged hourglasses, vases and baskets of fruit and flowers divided by bunches of laurel leaves tied up with ribbons and rosettes.

Caryatids, herms and terms

The idea of using human figures as columns to support doorways, porches and entablatures goes back to classical antiquity, and reminds us that the human figure is the ultimate guide to correct proportions in architecture. The ancient Roman architect Vitruvius wrote that naked, muscular male figures (*atlantes*) represented strength and virtue, while clothed male and female figures represented tribes conquered by the Greeks, supporting buildings as a sign of subjection. The female caryatid is named after the capture of the women of Caryae. Herms and terms were originally freestanding stones representing gods. Ancient Greek herms (*hermae*), representing Hermes, were placed at crossroads. The name is now usually applied to three-quarter-length figures without legs on short pedestals. Ancient Roman terms (*termini*) were boundary markers sacred to Terminus and are usually shown only as a head and upper torso on a longer pedestal. Since the 1500s herms and terms, like caryatids and atlantes, have been used as supports and framing devices both in architecture and the decorative arts.

IONIC AND CORINTHIAN TERMS
Low Countries, 1604
By Adrian Muntinck after Hindrich Muntinck
Engravings
2922& 4–1907
These terms show the close connection that was believed to exist between the human figure and the classical column. In the Corinthian terms the parts of the body are shown as architecture.

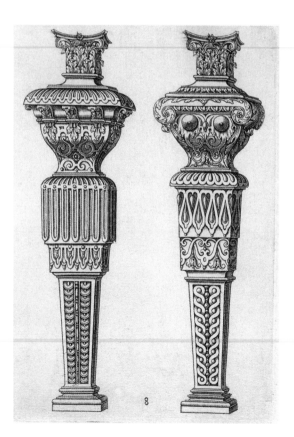

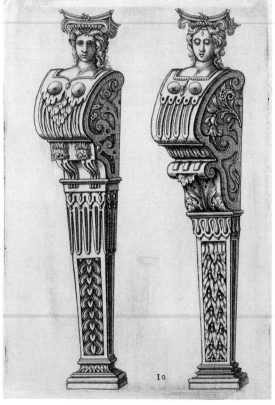

ERASMUS WITH A TERM

Swiss, about 1525
By Hans Lutzelbürger after Hans Holbein
Woodcut
14180

The famous scholar and theologian Desiderius Erasmus is shown with his hand on a freestanding figure of the god Terminus, his personal symbol of death. Architectural terms support the arch. The second edition of this print was used for the collected works of Erasmus, published in Basel in 1540.

PEDESTAL IN THE FORM OF A TERMINAL FIGURE OF A BOY

British, about 1730
Cast plaster, painted to imitate stone
W.5–1946

He supports an Ionic capital. Such pedestals would have been used in halls or garden buildings.

A PERFUME BURNER WITH CARYATIDS

Italian, about 1520–27
By Marco Dente after a design by Raphael
Engraving
29459.8

The perfume burner may have been for King François I of France, whose badge was the lizard-like salamander. The now-famous caryatids of the Erectheum in Athens were unknown in the sixteenth century – these caryatids are probably derived from Roman sculptures in the Greek style.

The vase

Pottery vases, made in different shapes, were the table, ceremonial and kitchen ware of the ancient Greeks. Highly decorated examples were placed in tombs, and soon certain types were being made in stone and other materials as pure decoration, very like vases today. For Renaissance designers, from about 1450, the vase became a powerful symbol of the classical past, and was widely used in buildings, gardens, interiors and on many other objects. Although they were mainly inspired by Roman stone examples, many new forms were invented, promoted by a huge number of vase prints. Even more prints were made during the period of Neo-classical 'vase mania' after about 1760. Greek pottery was rediscovered, copied by modern manufacturers, and used in the design of household objects. Certain famous stone vases, notably the Borghese, Medici and Warwick vases, gained cult status and were copied mechanically in different sizes and materials.

AN ICE PAIL IN THE FORM OF THE WARWICK VASE

British, about 1820
Probably made by Barr, Flight and Barr of Worcester Porcelain
C.467–1935 (Allen Bequest)

The enormous Warwick Vase, a Roman marble of the second century AD, was discovered in 1770 and restored in Rome by Giovanni Battista Piranesi, before being sold to the Earl of Warwick. It is now in the Burrell Collection, Glasgow. Thanks to Piranesi's print of it made in 1778, it was extensively copied and adapted, especially after about 1800. This highly simplified example keeps the characteristic twisted vine handles.

VASE

Italian, about 1490–1500
Made in the Marche,
perhaps at Pesaro
Tin-glazed earthenware
(maiolica)
351–1872 (Webb
Collection)

Vases of this shape, loosely similar to classical examples, were also made in bronze and appear in contemporary grotesque ornament and (from about 1450) in candelabrum decorations (see p.70). This example is decorated on the handles with money pattern and on the body with scalework and a grotesque.

SAUCE TUREEN

British, about 1790–1800
Copper plated with silver (Sheffield plate)
M.171–1912

In the second half of the eighteenth century the two-handled classical vase form influenced vessels of all types.

PRINT: VASES AND A CANDLESTICK AMONG ROMAN RUINS
German, 1675–9
By Cimmert after Joachim von Sandrart from his Teutsche Academie
Engraving
13630.1

Until the late seventeenth century designers had to rely on sixteenth-century prints for their knowledge of vases and other Roman objects. Here the vases so suggestively placed among ruins are taken from prints by Agostino Veneziano, Polidoro da Caravaggio and Enea Vico. None would now be mistaken for a real Roman object.

A BOY DRAWING
THE MEDICI VASE
Italian, 1656
By Stefano Della Bella
Etching
E.1527. A.528–1915

The Medici Vase, now in the Uffizi Gallery in Florence, is a Roman marble made about AD 50–100. It was at the Villa Medici in Rome by 1598. It was widely copied, often paired with the Borghese Vase. Here it is shown in the gardens of the villa: the boy may well be the Medici heir, later Grand Duke Cosimo III.

DESIGNS FOR VASES
French, 1639–48
By Stefano Della Bella
Etchings
29744.A.2

Della Bella's designs for vases had an immense influence, being copied by ceramic and other manufacturers up to the early 1800s. These prints come from the *Raccolta di vasi diversi*, published in Paris.

ARCHITECTURAL ORNAMENT: BREAKING THE RULES

About 1500, even as the classical orders were being made into a system of architectural law (see p.38), Italian architects and designers began to break the rules. The discovery of a type of fantastic ancient Roman wall decoration called the grotesque inspired a completely new type of ornament called strapwork. Islamic Moresque was added to it (p.72), allowing grotesque decoration to develop steadily over 250 years. A new emotional power was given to architecture by distorting and rearranging classical forms and inventing entirely new elements like the cartouche and baluster (pp.76 and 82). Strange new fleshy and rocky forms emerged from artificial garden grottoes. In the 1500s these developments produced a highly refined but slightly uneasy style called Mannerism, dominated by dense masses of ornament. In the 1600s a new and bolder architectural style called Baroque emerged in Italy (pp.78–80). The Baroque style used many Mannerist motifs but made them grander and more dramatic. It also developed its own type of naturalistic floral and acanthus ornament.

The grotesque: beginnings

About AD 30 the Roman architect Vitruvius criticized a type of painted wall decoration in which the classical orders were reduced to airy illogical structures inhabited by a strange collection of people, animals and fantastic creatures. Rediscovered about 1,500 years later, the paintings were called grotesques after the grotto-like buried rooms in which they were found, notably in the Golden House of Nero in Rome. Classical, yet without rules, the grotesque started an ornamental revolution. The grotesque was used for borders and fillers from about 1480, often together with the candelabrum (see pp.70–1). It was established as an ornamental system by Raphael, whose decorations of the Logge in the Vatican (1517–18) and the Villa Madama inspired prints that spread the idea to the rest of Europe. The strap-like elements used by Raphael developed into strapwork, prompting further departures from the ancient originals. The discovery of ancient paintings in the ruins of Pompeii and Herculaneum about 1750 led to a return to the Roman models as well as a new look at Raphael.

right
ROUNDEL
Italian, about 1510
Made in Siena
Tin-glazed earthenware (maiolica)
656–1884 (Castellani Collection)
The colours and composition of the grotesque on this roundel (of unknown use) are very similar to Bernardino Pinturicchio's decorations in the Piccolomini Library at Siena Cathedral, painted in 1503–8.

left

DETAIL OF THE DECORATION OF RAPHAEL'S LOGGE

Italian, 1772–7
By Giovanni Ottaviani after Pietro Camporesi and G. Savorelli
Hand-coloured etching
E.335–1887

The decorations of the second-floor logge, or open arcades, of the Vatican in Rome influenced European designers for 300 years. They were painted and modelled in stucco by Giovanni da Udine and others under the direction of Raphael in 1517–18. They established the grotesque, shown in the left panel here, as a European ornamental form. They also developed a highly influential type of light candelabrum ornament, here seen next to the grotesque, and the use of hanging naturalistic plant ornament.

TITLE-PAGE FOR A SET OF GROTESQUES

Italian, mid-16th century (originally published 1530–40)
By an anonymous engraver
Engraving
16770

The title in Latin reads 'light and (as can be seen) extemporized pictures which are commonly called grotesques which the ancient romans use for decorating dining rooms and other separate places of their houses which have been variously selected and faithfully and carefully reduced into one from many vaulted chambers and ancient walls'. The design is indeed close to Roman examples, and the set of prints was often republished and widely copied.

A GROTESQUE

Italian, 1525–50
By Nicoletto da Modena
Engraving
E.180–1885

Two of the figures on this print are copied from Nero's Golden House, where Nicoletto scratched his name in 1507. Soon afterwards the first edition of this print from a set of grotesques was published. In spite of this, the dense and imaginative style is not in fact close to the Roman original but much more like the earliest type of grotesque used by Bernardino Pinturicchio and other artists. Nicoletto's prints were among the first to show grotesques.

THE RUINS OF ANCIENT ROME
German, about 1560
By Virgil Solis of Nuremberg
Engravings
E.2862–4–1910 (Lanna Collection)

In these three imaginary scenes artists draw and measure the ruins. One view shows the type of buried building in which painted grotesque wall and ceiling decorations were found. These are reversed copies from a set of prints engraved by Jacques Androuet Ducerceau after Léonard Thiry, published in 1550.

Candelabrum ornament

The Roman candelabrum was a large stone candlestick made of piled-up decorative elements (see p.82). In the 1400s the same name was given to a type of classical ornament that used similar built-up elements to decorate a flat surface, usually a narrow upright panel, flanking a frame or forming a pilaster (a flat wall pillar). The candelabrum ornament used in Italy in the mid-1400s was quite simple in design and employed elements close to those of freestanding candelabra, especially vase and baluster shapes, from which plant-like elements appeared to grow. Towards the end of the 1400s a more elaborate type appeared with added figures, fantastic creatures, trophies of armour and other devices. This type was often used with the grotesque, and was influenced by it. The candelabrum was, however, always more controlled in design, never losing the basic idea of upward growth. In the early 1500s candelabrum ornament spread beyond Italy, pioneering the use of classical decoration in the rest of Europe.

right
A CANDELABRUM PILASTER
British, about 1851
Plaster cast
1851–240
This cast is taken from the monument of Louis XII of France in the abbey of St Denis, Paris, erected after his death in 1515. It shows an imaginary plant growing from a vase. The sculptors were the Giusti brothers from Italy, who used the simple candelabrum ornament invented in Florence in the 1400s.

PAGE WITH CANDELBRUM ORNAMENT

Swiss, 1515–16

By Urs Graf, from a book published by Johann Froben of Basel

Woodcut

29125.A

From the mid-1400s candelabrum ornament was used in Italy to decorate the pages of books. This page shows the Italian candelabrum entering Northern Europe through the work of the humanist publisher Froben .

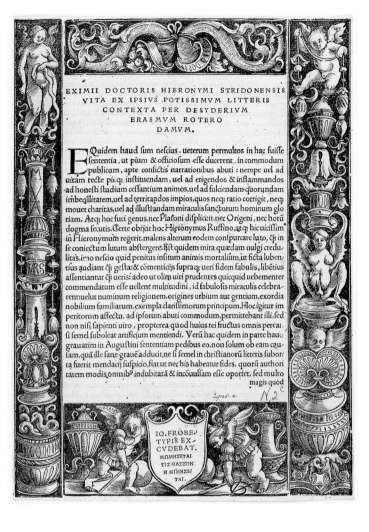

A CANDELABRUM

Italian, about 1505

By Giovanni Antonio da Brescia after Giovanni Pietro da Birago

Engraving

E.631–1890

With the discovery in the late 1400s of Roman grotesque wall painting, candelabra became more elaborate, using a wide range of different elements. The designer of this print, from a set of 12, was an illuminator. Such a complex composition could only have been done in paint, on a wall or on a decorated page.

The Moresque

The Moresque, named after the Moors, Muslims of North Africa and Spain, is also called the Arabesque. Like most Islamic ornament it is geometrical in design, using complex interlaced bands and tendrils from which little hook-shaped, leaf-like, forms spring. These knot-like patterns fascinated Renaissance painters, designers and craftsmen, who saw them on goods imported from Turkey and other Islamic countries. By about 1500 Moresque ornament was appearing in wall decorations. It was soon being used on bookbindings, textiles and manuscripts, ceramics and (from 1530) in ornament prints. About 1560 the Moresque invaded and became an essential part of the grotesque: the bands contributed to the development of strapwork (p.74–5), while the tendrils and leaf shapes kept some of their Islamic flavour. This has led to the term Arabesque being used in French to describe the grotesque.

TILE
Turkish, about 1420
Glazed earthenware
1038–1892
The leaves and tendrils of this type of Moresque were developed from the scrolls and palmettes of the ancient Greeks and Romans (pp.56–7)

PRINT: DESIGN FOR ENAMELLING
German, 1617
By Esaias van Hulsen
Published in Stuttgart
Engraving
E.3352–1928
The fantastic web of scrolls is inspired by the Moresque.

ENARRATIONUM IN PSALMOS, PARS PRIMA
1548
By Agostino Steuco
Published in Lyons by Sebastian Gryphius, probably bound in Paris.
Bound in calf with gold tooling
L.3395–1938

This book belonged to Jean Grolier, vicomte d'Aguisy, a notable collector who had the best finely produced books of his day bound to very 'avant-garde' designs by a number of different workshops. The design combines band work with leaves and tendrils. The central element of the strapwork and Moresque decoration is copied from a design in an embroidery pattern book by Giovanni Andrea Vavassore, *Esemplario di lavori* (Venice, 1530). Such embroidery prints were also used by silver engravers.

DESIGN FOR A EWER
German, 1579
Engraved by George Wechter
the Elder of Nuremberg
Engraving
E.4261–1910

In this design thick bands derived from the style of Fontainebleau (p.75) combine with others close to the Moresque. Wechter, who described himself as a painter, may have been responsible for introducing this type of dense all-over strapwork to goldsmiths' work. This print is from the set *30 Stück zum Verzachnen Für Die Goldschmid Verfertigt* ('30 Pieces for Drawing Prepared for the Goldsmith').

PLATE
Italian, dated 1537
Mark, painted in lustre: 'Mo Go', for Maestro Giorgio
Perhaps made in Castel Durante or Urbino, with lustre added at a final firing in the workshop of Maestro Giorgio Andreadi of Gubbio
Tin-glazed earthenware (maiolica)
6864–1860

The decoration is typical of the knot-work that so interested designers in the early sixteenth century. Similar patterns were used on Islamic-influenced pottery made in Spain and extensively exported.

The grotesque: strapwork

About 20 years after Raphael had systematized the grotesque (p.68), a new type of ornament emerged called strapwork. A typical product of the fantastic imagination of the Mannerist artist of the sixteenth century, it was invented by the painter Rosso Fiorentino for his decorations (made of modelled plaster) in the Gallery of François I at the palace of Fontainebleau. Its large leather-like scrolls and bands, often imprisoning human figures, were ideal for giving a sense of structure to otherwise borderless grotesques, and the motif was eagerly taken up and developed in the rest of Europe. The bands became narrower and from about 1560 combined with the Moresque, with its complex interlace patterns (pp.72–3). The centre for this development was Antwerp, where designers and printmakers added their own weird and comic distortions (p.76). From about 1680 French designers, led by Jean Berain, returned to the strapwork grotesque of the previous century; as *laub und bandelwerk* (leaf and strapwork) it became the leading form of Northern European ornament up to about 1730.

TOILET POT AND COVER
French, about 1700–20
Made in the Saint-Cloud factory
Porcelain, painted in blue
C.478–1909 (J.H. Fitzhenry Gift)
This pot is decorated with strapwork lambrequins (French: heraldic mantling), which had been popularized by the grotesque compositions of Jean Berain. The colours are intended to recall Chinese porcelain.

PELEAS KILLED BY HIS DAUGHTERS
French, 1563
Engraved by René Boyvin after Léonard Thiry
Engraving
26595.E
The strapwork border is in the style devised for the palace at Fountainebleau, where Thiry worked as a painter under Rosso. The scene is from the story of Jason and the Golden Fleece; it is plate 23 from *Hystoria Iasonis*, published in Paris in 1563.

A GROTESQUE
French, about 1685–93
Engraved by Jean Dolivar after Jean Berain
Engraving
29876.4
This print, which probably shows a tapestry design, is characteristic of Jean Berain's clearly defined interlacing strapwork. The subject is Cupid; other prints in the set from which it comes show classical gods and goddesses.

ORNAMENTAL FRAME

Low Countries, about 1590–1600
Engraved by Nicolaes de Bruyn after Hans Vredeman de Vries
Engraving
E.1413–1923 (Rosenheim Collection)

This engraving is copied from a set of prints designed by the Antwerp designer Hans Vredeman de Vries, published in 1569. His prints had an enormous influence in spreading the strapwork style across Europe.

PRINT: *MERCURY*

Low Countries, about 1590
Engraved by Adiaen Collaert of Antwerp from a set illustrating the Judgement of Paris.
Engraving
E.2440–1912

The grotesque became ever lighter and more complex towards the end of the sixteenth century, using strapwork that had completely absorbed the thick bands of Fontainebleau, as well as the Moresque.

Cartouches and fleshy forms

An interest in the strange and fantastic, long a feature of European ornament, became particularly marked from about 1550. A new type of ornament was invented in Antwerp that used certain kinds of natural forms: the gristly parts of fishes, shells, and fleshy and scaly shapes. These emerged from the fashion for grottoes, artificial caves inhabited by sculptures of snakes, frogs, fish and other creatures. Their walls imitated or incorporated moss, natural rock and dripping water. The fleshy style became international about 1600, and is called auricular, after the shapes of the ear. Although auricular ornament ceased to be widely popular after about 1660, it continued in use on cartouches. The cartouche form, which was unknown to the Greeks and Romans, had appeared by the early 1500s as a frame or shield with edges that recalled curled paper. From about 1620 cartouches began to be asymmetrical, a daring departure from the classical rules that became a vital part of the Baroque and Rococo styles (see pp.78–81).

TAPESTRY PANEL SHOWING A CARTOUCHE
French, 1878
Made by the pupils of the National Manufactory of the Gobelins
Woven with coloured worsteds on string warps
30–1879 (part)
This exhibition piece returns to the curled-paper origins of the cartouche. It was given to the South Kensington Museum by Monsieur Bardoux, French Minister of Education, Religion and Fine Arts.

A FANTASY SCENE
Low Countries, 1556
Engraved by Lucas or Johannes Duetecum after Cornelis Floris
Published in Antwerp by Hieronymus Cock
Engraving
29170.7
Cornelis Floris was a leading Antwerp architect and sculptor who helped to pioneer strapwork (pp.74–5) as well as the fleshy style. This print may depict the type of fantastic wagon used in carnival processions. It comes from the set *Veelderley Veranderinghe van grotissen ende Compertimenten . . . Libro Primo* ('Many Variations of Grottoes and Compartments . . . Book One').

A CARTOUCHE ENCLOSING A LANDSCAPE
French, about 1625
Etched by Daniel Rabel, from the set Cartouches
de different inventions
Etching
20321.1

Rabel's cartouche prints helped to introduce the
auricular style to France. Here the curling edges
have the character of dried fish, while a fishy
mask and horse's skull peer out.

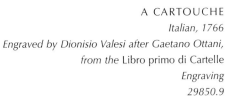

DISH
British, London hallmarks for 1772–3
Mark of John Parker and Edward Wakelin
Silver gilt
7241–1861

This dish was made for the 3rd Duke of Chandos (died 1789) to make a pair
with a South German dish of about 1630–50. The auricular ornament
incorporates masks and monsters. It was probably carried out by one of the
several German chasers working in eighteenth-century London.

A CARTOUCHE
Italian, 1766
Engraved by Dionisio Valesi after Gaetano Ottani,
from the Libro primo di Cartelle
Engraving
29850.9

Violently unbalanced, this is an extreme example
of a Baroque asymmetrical cartouche. Such
cartouches were especially popular among mural
and theatrical painters such as Ottani, who used
the Baroque style almost to the end of the
eighteenth century.

Mannerism and Baroque

From the 1530s in Italy the rules of the classical orders began to be broken by architects and designers. Michelangelo and Giulio Romano began to give architecture a new emotional power by distorting and rearranging classical forms and emphasizing their more dramatic devices, such as the rough stonework of rustication. In the resulting Mannerist architecture (Italian, *maniera*: style) the classical orders developed into new forms, often using strapwork and other grotesque ornaments. Prints spread Mannerism to Northern Europe, where the dense masses of surface decoration were especially popular. The Baroque style, which began in Italy in the early 1600s, may derive its name from the Spanish word for a misshapen pearl. Using many Mannerist motifs, it was marked by a greatly developed tendency to the grand and theatrical. The twisted Salomonic column, with its sense of space and movement, is a typical motif.

below

THE PORTA PIA, ROME
Italian, 1635
Illustration from Giacomo Barozzio
da Vignola's Regola delli cinque
ordini d'architettura
Engraving
62 C 53

The Porta Pia gateway, designed by Michelangelo in 1561, is a typical sixteenth-century fantasy on the theme of classical architecture. It mixes Doric and Tuscan orders, as well as having both a triangular pediment and a broken scrolled one. The unsettling effect of the distortions of scale is emphasized by the screaming mask. Vignola's influential book on the orders was first published in 1562.

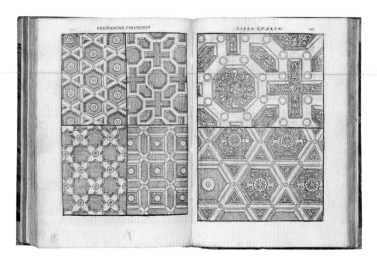

THE 'FIVE BOOKS OF ARCHITECTURE' AND THE *LIBRO ESTRAORDINARIO*
1566
By Sebastiano Serlio
Published in Venice by Francesco Senese and
Zuane Krugher
87 E 31

In his book Serlio recorded some of the many types of contemporary wooden ceilings that were developed by architects out of the much simpler Roman coffering, or sunk panelling. Serlio's illustrations spread such designs very widely: by 1611 editions of his book had been published in French, German, Dutch, Flemish and English.

A RUSTICATED WINDOW IN THE TUSCAN ORDER

German, 1598
By Wendel Dietterlin
Etching
28766.18

Rustication, the use in building of prominent roughly finished stones, was invented by the Romans. It was eagerly taken up and developed by sixteenth-century architects who contrasted its lack of sophistication (*rus*, Latin: the country) with more refined architectural forms. This print comes from Dietterlin's *Architectura*, published in Nuremberg.

A BUFFET AND A CUPBOARD

Low Countries, 1630
Anonymous engraver after
Paul Vredeman de Vries
Engraving
E.3740–1953

This print shows Mannerist variations on the classical orders, here applied to furniture. Hans Vredeman de Vries and his son Paul played a major part in bringing this type of Mannerist design to Northern Europe. This print is from the set *Verscheyden Schrynwerck*, published in Amsterdam.

A SALOMONIC COLUMN

Italian, mid-16th century
Engraved by Nicolas Beatrizet
Engraving
E.2393–1913

This print, published in Rome, shows the 'Colonna Santa', a twisted bronze column in St Peter's. It was believed to be one of the two columns called Jachin and Boaz that had stood at the gate of the Temple of Jerusalem built by Solomon (and was therefore called Salomonic). After being shown by Raphael in one of his designs for tapestries (1515–16), the spiral form became a favourite way of breaking the classical rules, particularly for Baroque designers, who were also inspired by Bernini's Baldacchino in St Peter's (1624–33), which was held up by four huge Salomonic columns. The 'Colonna Santa' is in fact Roman, and was made in the Eastern Empire in the early second century AD.

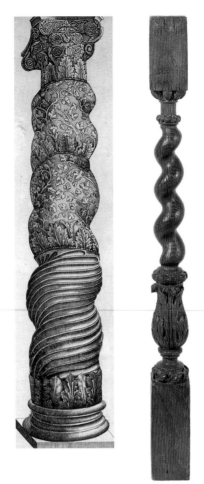

BALUSTER IN THE FORM OF A SALOMONIC COLUMN

English, about 1700
Oak
664a–1906

After the Salomonic form had been used by Bernini in the Baldacchino at St Peter's, it became a favourite element in Baroque design.

A TRIUMPHAL ARCH ON THE LOUVRE

French, 1704
Engraved by René Charpentier and Nicolas Chevallier after Charpentier
Engraving
27935

This print shows the Baroque decorations celebrating the birth of the Duke of Burgundy, set up on the façade of the Louvre palace in Paris. Designed by the sculptor François Girardon, they incorporated the existing columns in the French Doric order built by Jacques II Androuet Ducerceau in 1603. Invented by Philibert de l'Orme, the French orders interrupted the column shaft with thick rings, making it easier to construct out of several blocks of stone.

Decoration du grand pavillon des galeries du Louvre faite par les soins et du dessein du S.ʳ Girardon Sculpteur ordinaire du Roy le 28. aoust 1704 jour de la feste donnée par la ville de Paris pour la naissance de MONSEIGNEUR le Duc de Bretagne.

Rococo and *rocaille*

The word Rococo comes from rocaille, the shell and rock work used in garden grottoes from the 1500s onwards (see p.76). The Rococo style, with its sense of intimacy, fantasy and movement, began in France in the early eighteenth century with a lightening of the classical grotesque (p.75). From the 1720s it matured into the genre pittoresque, a style largely invented by the goldsmith, designer and architect Juste Aurèle Meissonier. The dominating rocaille was combined with vigorous 'S'- and 'C'-shaped scrolls, vases, cartouches and fantastic figures, all composed with a strong lack of symmetry. Meissonnier also invented a new form of ornament, the morceau de fantaisie (piece of fantasy), a type of dream structure inspired by the classical grotesque as well as Italian Baroque architectural and theatre-set design. The Rococo style spread quickly from France to the rest of Europe. From the 1750s it was gradually replaced by the sterner Greek and Roman forms of Neo-classicism, but was revived in the 1820s.

THE FROZEN FOUNTAIN
French, 1736
Engraved by Jean Baptiste Guélard after Jacques de La Joue
Engraving
29678.3
This is one of the earliest printed examples of a *morceau de fantaisie*. In addition to rocaille there is frozen water, another favourite Rococo motif. It comes from the set *Livre nouveau de douze morceaux de fantaisie utiles à divers usages* ('New Book of Twelve Pieces of Fantasy Useful for Different Purposes').

TEA KETTLE AND STAND
British, London hallmarks for 1753–4
Mark of William Grundy
Silver
918&a–1905
The body and stand are decorated with 'C' and 'S' scrolls, *rocaille*, shells and flower garlands.

AN ESSAY ON THE WRITINGS AND GENIUS OF SHAKESPEARE
1770
By Elizabeth Montagu
Published in London by J. and H. Hughes, 1770. The binding possibly done through James Bate, stationer of London
In a contemporary gold-tooled tree-calf binding
AM 163–1964
The Rococo grotesque ornament, taken from a print by Johann Ernst Baumgarten, includes a Chinaman and the lion and unicorn supporters of the British Royal Arms. Similar grotesques can be found on many other British objects of this period, from tombstones to trade cards.

Balusters and candelabra

All the objects shown here are descendants of the ancient Roman candelabrum, a tall holder for a *candela* or wax taper. Especially remarkable were the large marble candelabra made for temples and palaces, composed of piled-up bulb-shaped and other decorative elements. From the early 1400s they not only helped to inspire the flat decoration known as candelabrum ornament (see p.70–1), but also survived long enough as a standard type to influence the design of street lamps. The candelabrum was also the basis of the baluster, which supports the railing of the balustrade on staircases and balconies. Unknown to the ancient Romans, the balustrade first appeared in the later 1400s. Even when turned into the banisters of modern staircases, the classical inspiration of the baluster is quite obvious.

BALUSTER
FROM A
STAIRCASE
*Low Countries, late
17th century
Oak
604–1883*
This type of double-bulbed baluster was one of the first to become popular in the early 1400s. The resemblance between the clasping acanthus leaves and the pomegranate flower gave the baluster its name (*balustro*, Italian: pomegranate flower).

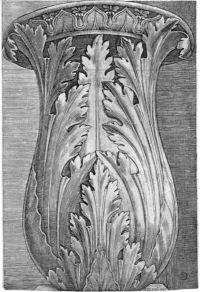

A ROMAN CANDELABRUM
*Italian, about 1550
By an anonymous engraver
Published in Rome by Antonio Salamanca
Engraving
14891*
This shows part of a famous candelabrum in the church of Sant'Agnese in Rome. A candelabrum was made by piling up several such parts. The print has been cut at the bottom.

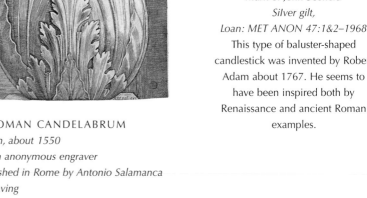

CANDLESTICK
*British, London hallmarks for
1791–2 and 1792–3
Mark of John Scofield
Silver gilt,
Loan: MET ANON 47:1&2–1968*
This type of baluster-shaped candlestick was invented by Robert Adam about 1767. He seems to have been inspired both by Renaissance and ancient Roman examples.

Nº 50. Nº 43. Nº 51. Nº 40. Nº 52. Nº 45. Nº 46. Nº 48. Nº 44. Nº 47.

PATTERNS FOR LAMP-POSTS

German, about 1890

Lithograph

E.1148–1965

When designing lamp-posts people naturally turn to candlesticks and candelabra for inspiration. This sheet is from a trade catalogue.

LOOKING OUT AND LOOKING BACK

The ancient Greeks and Romans developed a language of ornament that was rich and flexible, but highly structured: this became the leading language of European architecture and decoration after about 1450. There were, however, always rebellions against the classical orders and rules, and attempts to create new and imaginative styles. In their hunt for new ideas, some looked outside Europe for inspiration, to countries such as India, China and Egypt, while others looked back into Europe's own medieval past. These exotic and historic styles were also examined and recorded for their own sakes, culminating in the many nineteenth-century encyclopaedias of ornament (p.15) that interpreted such styles as governed by rules just as strict as those of classicism. Treated now with a greater seriousness, the ornamental forms of almost the whole world and most past periods were plundered to feed the insatiable desire for new motifs. New inspiration was discovered in Japan, while in the twentieth century tribal art became an important source of ornament.

China

Luxury goods from China, especially silks, have long been known and prized in Europe. In turn Chinese ornament has absorbed Western motifs such as the palmette (pp.56–7). Once Vasco da Gama had opened up the sea route to China in 1498, ever-increasing quantities of blue and white porcelain, lacquer ware, wallpaper and other novelties were produced for the West. Cheaper copies were also made in Europe. These soon went beyond direct imitation and the playful imaginative style known as Chinoiserie was born. Sometimes this focused on recognizable individual motifs, such as latticework or bamboo. More often it was an excuse to wander in a vaguely exotic dream world, inspired by Indian as well as Chinese art and untroubled by the rules governing classical ornament. Here you could find 'a Butterfly supporting an Elephant, or Things equally absurd: yet . . . their gay Colouring and Airy Disposition seldom fail to please' (Jean Pillement, 1758). The style was especially favoured by Rococo designers (p.81), and is still popular today.

WILLOW PATTERN PLATE
British, about 1991
Made by the Churchill Pottery, Stoke-on-Trent
Earthenware, transfer-printed
C.247–1991 (Given by Michael Snodin)
The Willow Pattern is one of the world's most popular decorations for ceramics. It is not a real Chinese design, but a fanciful assembly of Chinoiserie motifs, although it is influenced by the decoration of Chinese ceramics made for export to Europe. The pattern is believed to have been invented by Thomas Minton about 1780; the 'old Chinese tale' that it is supposed to illustrate did not appear until 1849.

right
STANDISH (INKSTAND)
British, London hallmarks 1758–9
Mark of S. Herbert & Co.
Silver, with glass ink-pots
M.105–1940 (Arthur Hurst Bequest)
'Chinese fret' patterns like that which surrounds this standish were an important element of eighteenth-century Chinoiserie decoration, found on garden buildings and furniture as well as silver.

TANKARD

*English, London hallmarks for 1670–71
(body) and 1671–2 (lid)
Marks of RH with cinquefoil on body,
and DH with a rose on lid
Silver
36–1865*

The flat chased decoration is typical of
Chinoiserie decoration on late
seventeenth-century British silver,
mixing Italian fountains, Persian
soldiers and other elements with
Chinese birds, flowers and trees. The
shape of the tankard remains resolutely
European.

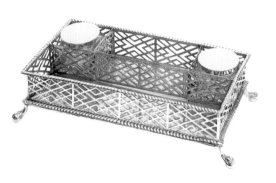

DESIGN FOR A CHINA CABINET

*Dutch, about 1700
Etched by Daniel Marot
Etching
E.1672.20–1888*

Blue and white Chinese porcelain became highly fashionable in Europe.
By the end of the seventeenth century, it was being imported in large
quantities and European copies in tin-glazed earthenware were also
available. Here it is loaded onto shelves and brackets in a small room, and
even placed within the fireplace. The walls have also apparently been
japanned in imitation of East Asian lacquer.

Japan

Japan deliberately restricted its contacts with the West until the 1850s. Its carefully guarded isolation meant that Japanese influence on European ornament, with the exception of ceramics, had been very limited compared to that of China. As the market opened up, this excitingly unfamiliar culture would become a major influence on Western design for the rest of the century. Displays of Japanese art at the International Exhibitions in London in 1862 and in Paris in 1867 attracted much interest and admiration. The contrast between over-ornamented European products and Japanese simplicity was a formative influence on the artists and designers of the new Aesthetic Movement, such as E.W. Godwin, Walter Crane and James Whistler. Imported goods were soon available through specialist dealers such as Liberty, and many illustrated books on Japan appeared in the 1870s and '80s. These included guides to its ornament: the striking asymmetry and the flat, clearly defined lines and colours were easy to imitate. Motifs such as chrysanthemums, cranes and fans became very popular.

VASE
British, 1870–80
Made by Elkington & Co.,
Birmingham
Cloisonné enamel on gilt copper
1276a–1886 (Dixon Bequest)
Both the decorative enamel technique and the choice of motifs were influenced by Japanese examples of the time.

CLOCK
British, about 1880
Designed by Lewis F. Day
Made by Howell James &
Co. of London
Ebonized wood case and
porcelain face
Circ.662–1972
The ebonized case of this clock, with its fretwork decoration, and the flowers on its face have little to do with real Japanese decoration, but would instantly have suggested the Japanese taste to Day's contemporaries. Lewis F. Day was an influential teacher and prolific designer, whose books frequently included Japanese examples (see p.17).

SWEETMEAT STAND
British, about 1755
Made at the Bow factory, London
Porcelain, painted in enamel colours and gilded
C.986–1924 (E.F. Broderip Gift)
The decoration and the shape of the three small dishes are obviously influenced by a Japanese dish like the Kakiemon saucer shown here. The chrysanthemum-flower shape of the original has been squashed to form a shell.

SAUCER
Japanese, about 1700
Made in the Arita distict, Saga Prefecture
Porcelain, painted in enamel colours and gilded (Kakiemon ware)
C.2–1936
In the seventeenth and eighteenth centuries, trade with Japan was restricted to Japanese and Chinese merchants operating through the port of Nagasaki. From there large quantities of porcelain were exported to Europe. Kakiemon wares like this saucer were especially sought after. Kakiemon ware is named after Sakaida Kakiemon, who is traditionally credited with making the first porcelain in Japan in 1643.

Egypt and Africa

The ancient and mysterious civilization of Egypt had a powerful influence on those of Greece and Rome, and continues to fascinate the West. Single motifs such as obelisks and hieroglyphs have been in use since the Renaissance, inspired by imported objects and travellers' tales. In the eighteenth century, designers such as Giovanni Battista Piranesi pioneered the use of a complete Egyptian style. This became better known (and more accurate) when systematic explorations and excavations began at the end of the century. The ancient Egyptians' concern with death and ritual meant that the style was especially useful for cemeteries and Masonic halls, but more general outbreaks of 'Egyptomania' were prompted by events like the battle of the Nile in 1798, the opening of the Suez Canal in 1869 and the discovery of Tutankhamen's tomb in 1922. Owen Jones's *Grammar of Ornament* (1856) included examples of the 'Ornament of Savage Tribes', but Europe only began to take black African culture seriously in the early twentieth century. Tribal art has been an increasingly popular source of Western ornament since the 1920s.

PAIR OF ANKLE SOCKS
British, 1990
Made for the Sock Shop
Cotton, nylon polyamide and elasthane
T.178/1&2–1991 (Given by Michael Snodin)
The bright colours and the masks on these socks are drawn from African art.

FURNISHING FABRIC
British, 1923
Made by F. Steiner & Co.
Roller-printed cotton
Circ.458–1966
Howard Carter's sensational discovery of Tutankhamen's tomb in 1922 brought the Egyptian style back into fashion.

TEAPOT

British, about 1810

Made by the Wedgwood factory

Red stoneware ('rosso antico' ware) with applied relief decoration in black

2375&a–1901

This teapot is from a range of 'hieroglyphic' ware developed by Josiah Wedgwood II in the early nineteenth century. It is decorated with an assortment of Egyptian motifs, including crocodiles and the winged disc associated with the gods Horus and Edfu.

Culte d'Ibis

L' Immortalité de l'Âme

Zwen Egyptische Vasen von Porphir Vier Spannen hoch, dem Marches del Carpio Vice-König von Napoli gehörig. Aus.

Deux Vases de Porphyre Egyptiens hauts de quatre Palmes, apartenans au Marquis del Carpio Viceroi de Naples.

TWO VASES

Austrian, 1721

Engraved by I.A. Delsenbach after Johann Bernhard Fischer von Erlach

Engraving

27914.3

This print is from Fischer von Erlach's comparative history of architecture, published in Vienna in 1721. Although the two vases are described as genuine Egyptian antiquities, they are in fact fanciful concoctions in the auricular style (see p.77).

Islam and India

In the eighth century AD the great Islamic empire founded by Muhammad stretched from central Asia to Spain. It soon disintegrated, but many of its peoples continued to share a common faith, outlook and culture. The Koranic tradition forbids the use of images of men and animals, and symbols, so geometrical and floral motifs are particularly characteristic of Islamic ornament. Silks and rugs from the Near and Middle East have long been highly prized and imitated in Europe, while about the year 1500 interlacing Moresque patterns were absorbed into European ornament (pp.72–3). Brightly coloured Indian textiles were also available about 1600, and typical motifs like the Paisley and the Tree of Life were soon being copied. In addition, places such as India and Persia were often seen as dream countries like China, and inspired similar fantasies. In the nineteenth century the search for new styles promoted a detailed analysis of the arts of India and Islam, through works such as Owen Jones's pioneering study of the ornament of the Alhambra in Granada (published 1842–5).

The tulip and carnation patterns on imported Iznik ceramics from Turkey had considerable influence on European ceramic decoration. This is an exceptionally close imitation, although the potter has not been able to match the brilliant blues and red of the original.

The ornament on this is taken from Persian illuminated manuscripts; Owen Jones included similar borders in his *Grammar of Ornament*. Appropriately, this card was designed for a banquet commemorating the Paris International Exhibition in 1867; such exhibitions did much to stimulate interest in non-European styles of ornament.

The delicate and complex Islamic decoration of the fourteenth-century palace of the Alhambra in Spain inspired the Alhambresque style of the nineteenth century, which is especially associated with Owen Jones. This is a model of one of the large side arches in the Hall of Comares.

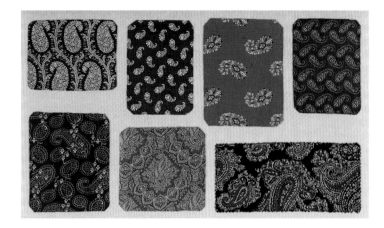

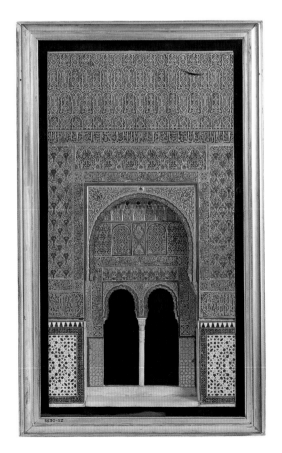

SAMPLES OF PAISLEY PATTERNS

British and French, mid-19th century
Printed dress cotton
T.67.B49–1957

These samples are taken from a collection assembled by a Macclesfield silk designer. All of them show the hook-shaped *boteh* or paisley motif. Its origins are obscure, but it is found throughout the East, and is especially associated with India. In the mid-nineteenth century it became a popular pattern for European fabrics, especially shawls. The pattern's name derives from the wool-weaving town of Paisley in Scotland, where many shawls were produced.

'ZODIAC' BISCUIT TIN

British, 1937
Made by Huntley, Boorne & Stevens for Huntley & Palmers
Tin plate, offset litho printed
M.437–1983 (M.J. Franklin Collection)

This tin is decorated with a fashionable jumble of Indian, East Asian and European Art Deco motifs. On the side are the signs of the zodiac. The dancing figure is using a cocktail shaker.

The medieval revival

Gothic was the last architectural style of the European Middle Ages; it was superseded from about 1450 onwards by the classical style of the Renaissance. The Gothic style did not arouse much interest again until the 1740s, when pointed arches, fan vaulting and other motifs were used in Britain to create a picturesque 'Gothick', closely related to the Rococo (p.81). In the nineteenth century a more historically accurate Gothic style became one of the major options in the huge range of available ornamental styles. Its historical and religious associations gave it an important advantage. Looking still further back in time, Celtic interlace patterns were associated with the rebirth of national culture in Ireland and Scotland. Similar forms also appeared in Russia and Scandinavia. Their sinuous lines contributed to the development of the Art Nouveau style.

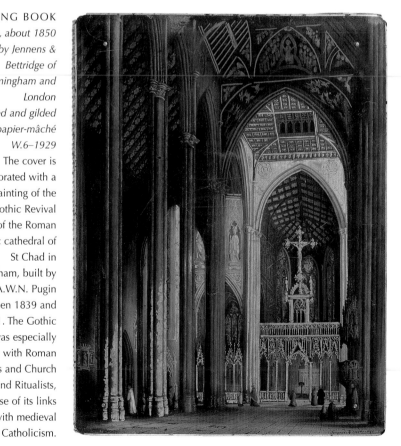

BLOTTING BOOK
British, about 1850
Made by Jennens &
Bettridge of
Birmingham and
London
Painted and gilded
papier-mâché
W.6–1929
The cover is decorated with a painting of the Gothic Revival interior of the Roman Catholic cathedral of St Chad in Birmingham, built by A.W.N. Pugin between 1839 and 1841. The Gothic style was especially popular with Roman Catholics and Church of England Ritualists, because of its links with medieval Catholicism.

CANDLESTICK
British, Sheffield hallmark for
1773–4
Mark of Samuel Roberts & Co.
Silver
843b–1905
The eighteenth-century approach to Gothic, exemplified by books such as Batty Langley's *Gothic Architecture Improved by Rules and Proportions* (1747), was less than accurate. The stem of this candlestick resembles Langley's Gothic columns, but the decoration on the base is Neo-classical. Standard dimensions made the bases and stems of such candlesticks interchangeable.

PLANT-POT HOLDER
British, about 1851
Designed by A.W.N. Pugin
Made by Minton and Co.
Earthenware tiles with block-printed decoration;
gilded cast-iron mounts
926–1852
Pugin was a central figure in the Gothic Revival of the mid-nineteenth century. This piece was shown in the Great Exhibition of 1851: the floriated decoration on the tiles includes fleurs-de-lis (stylized lilies) and quatrefoils (motifs like rosettes with four petals).

PRESENTATION
ADDRESS
*Irish, dated June
1877
Illuminated
manuscript
MS.L.69/2–1984*
The Irish shamrock and interlace patterns derived from medieval manuscripts dominated Celtic Revival decoration.

BALUSTER PANEL
American, 1899–1901
*Designed by Louis
Henry Sullivan
Cast iron
M.31–1972*
This Gothic Revival panel was made for the Carson, Pirie Scott & Co. building in Chicago. Sullivan used a Gothic style that greatly developed its organic characteristics.

Further reading

The literature on Western ornament is huge. This is a sample only from the more basic materials for further study – a fuller list of these is given in Snodin and Howard, cited below. In addition to specialized books and articles, much information on ornament can also be found in studies of prints, the decorative arts and architecture.

Dorothy Bosomworth, *The Encyclopaedia of Patterns and Motifs: a Collection of 5000 Designs from Cultures around the World*, London, 1995

Stuart Durant, *Ornament: a Survey of Decoration since 1830*, London and Sydney, 1986

Joan Evans, *Pattern: a study of Ornament in Western Europe from 1180 to 1900*, Oxford, 1931

John Fleming and Hugh Honour, *The Penguin Dictionary of the Decorative Arts*, Harmondsworth, 1977

Peter Fuhring, *Design into Art. Drawings for Architecture and Ornament: the Lodewijk Houthakker Collection*, London, 1989

E.H. Gombrich, *The Sense of Order: a Study in the Psychology of Decorative Art*, London, 1979

Alain Gruber (ed.), *A History of the Decorative Arts*, New York, 1994

George L. Hersey, *The Lost Meaning of Classical Architecture: Speculations on Ornament from Vitruvius to Venturi*, Cambridge, Mass., and London, 1988

Simon Jervis, *The Penguin Dictionary of Design and Designers*, Harmondsworth, 1984

Owen Jones, *The Grammar of Ornament*, London, 1856 (modern reprints include Studio Editions, 1986, Parkgate Books, 1997)

Philippa Lewis and Gillian Darley, *Dictionary of Ornament*, London, 1985

F.S. Meyer, *Handbook of Ornament*, London, 1888 (1892 edition reprinted by Dover, 1957, etc.)

Jessica Rawson, *Chinese Ornament: the Lotus and the Dragon*, London, 1984

Michael Snodin and Maurice Howard, *Ornament: a Social History Since 1450*, London, 1996

Peter Thornton, *Form and Decoration: Innovation in the Decorative Arts, 1470–1870*, London, 1998

James Trilling, *The Language of Ornament*, London, 2001

James Trilling, *Ornament: A Modern Perspective*, London, 2003

Peter Ward-Jackson, 'Some Mainstreams and Tributaries in European Ornament from 1500 to 1750', *Victoria and Albert Museum Bulletin* (3), 1967, pp.58ff, 90ff, 121ff

Eva Wilson, *8000 Years of Ornament: an Illustrated Handbook of Motifs*, London, 1994

Jonathan M. Woodham, *Twentieth-century Ornament*, London, 1990

Index